Impelled by the of Love of Christ

The Life and Ministry
of the
Sisters of Charity of Nazareth
1924-1936

Patricia Kelley, SCN and Rachel Willet, SCN

ISBN 0-925928-25-9

Printing by Art-Print & Publishing Company

©2011
Sisters of Charity of Nazareth

Cover Design by Katy Keeslar, Keeslar Creative
Book Design by Brad Craig

Dedication

To the Sisters of Charity of Nazareth of 1924–1936
whose lives and ministries met the challenges of their times
and set precedents for future ministries.

Contents

Foreword

The congregation of the Sisters of Charity of Nazareth was founded in Nelson County, Kentucky on December 1, 1812. The history of the first one hundred years, entitled *The Sisters of Charity of Nazareth, Kentucky*, written by Nazareth Academy Alumna, Anna Blanche McGill, was published in 1917. To honor the congregation on the occasion of its two-hundredth anniversary in 2012, a series entitled *Impelled by the Love of Christ*, is being published. The first book covered the life of Mother Rose Meagher and the events of her administration from 1912-1924. This second book in the series continues SCN history from 1924-1936 under the leadership of Mother Mary Catharine Malone.

Mother Mary Catharine reaffirmed the practice, begun by her predecessor, of naming an annalist in each local community whose duty it was to record significant happenings at her mission. In a circular letter Mother concluded: "I urge all concerned to take an active interest in preserving for future generations the history of our beloved community, trusting it will continue to be, as it has been in the past, a record of God's mercy and loving protection."

Most annalists realized the importance of their task. The following is a unique entry written in 1912 and found in the annals of St. Ann Convent, Portland Ave., Louisville, Kentucky:

Few will know we lived a hundred years from now! So the poet sings, but we of St. Ann's wish the sisters who come after us, a hundred years from now... to know something about the first sisters of this little branch of the great parent tree, Nazareth. We want them to know how we lived in the twentieth century. Well, dear annalist of the year 2012, we will tell our story, simple though it be....

In 1924, Mother Mary Catharine approved the establishment and maintenance of a system of permanent records for each sister. The card contains personal information regarding the family of the sister, dates of birth, entry into the congregation, profession of vows, names and dates of mission assignments, and date of death. From the annals and from these permanent record cards, the authors gathered the valuable information used in the preparation of this manuscript.

The materials used in this book came from the Archives of the Sisters of Charity of Nazareth and the oral history from sisters living today who knew Mother Mary Catharine. The authors gratefully acknowledge the assistance of Frances Krumpelman, SCN, Brother Joel McGraw, F.S.C., Marilyn Shea, SCN, and J. Emmanuel Willett, Ph.D, for reading the manuscript and offering helpful comments; Kathy Hertel-Baker, Nazareth archivist and Anna Powell, assistant archivist; Elaine McCarron, SCN, editor; and the Publications Committee: Mary Serra Goethals, SCN, chair, Mary Medley Bonn, Maureen Coughlin, SCN, and Margaret Rodericks, SCN, for editing assistance in preparing this manuscript for publication.

Chapter One

Biography
and Early Events

The welcoming party of Sisters of Charity of Nazareth, waiting outside the small Nazareth railway station to greet SCNs coming home, felt the rise of the summer heat that morning in July 1924. Some used collapsible fans to stir a breeze; others used stiff fans donated by a wholesale grocer; still others more gracefully dabbed their foreheads and chins, all to keep their linen collars fresh.

A distant whistle announced the approach of the southbound Louisville and Nashville (L&N) 9 a.m. train. For the sisters on board the arriving train, fatigue gave way to joy and enthusiasm as they anticipated greeting friends again. Most of the travelers were coming to participate in the fourth General Chapter of the Congregation, while others were coming for summer school or for rest and relaxation. A louder whistle cut through the plumes of smoke rising from the locomotive until a screech of brakes brought the train to a halt.

Nazareth's faithful Tom Tobin, as tall and lanky as Abraham Lincoln, visualized the mountain of luggage soon to be his charge to take to the motherhouse. The sisters entrusted their luggage to Tom, but each guardedly held on to her own black cardboard cap box, a treasure for any traveling SCN. Within it was a clean, starched, pinned-into-shape, ready-to-wear white cap. The white cap evolved from the Kentucky sunbonnet worn in 1812 by the foundress, Catherine Spalding, and pioneer women of the era. Worn with loyal dignity for more than a century, the white cap became the identifying mark of Sisters of Charity of Nazareth.

The sisters paired off for the half mile walk to the motherhouse where doors were open to welcome them. Mother Rose Meagher and her Council, and others who could be there, warmly greeted the travelers in traditional Southern style. The atmosphere in the front hall was charged with the joy of reunion. The delegates had come to choose a new leader, the third Mother General to be elected since 1911 when the congregation had received papal approbation. Dinner conversation became an exchange of small talk, news, and good-natured teasing as memories surfaced of days when sisters had been missioned together. Prayers that day included the community novena to St. Vincent de Paul and special intercessions for guidance of the Holy Spirit during the upcoming General Chapter.

The arriving delegates, coming from academies and schools, orphanages and hospitals as distant as Massachusetts and as close as Louisville, shared the exciting newness of the 1920s. Their awareness of implications for change and progress ushered in by the expanded use of the railway, the automobile, the airplane, the telephone, and the radio made for enthusiastic repartee as the younger "home community" absorbed information shared by veterans from the various missions.

On July 19, 1924, confident that the Holy Spirit would direct their proceedings, in prayerful silence and serious demeanor, the ninety-five delegates entered the community room at the motherhouse, the hall of elections. Most Reverend John A. Floersh, Bishop of Louisville, the youngest bishop in the United States of America at the time, presided at the election of Mother Mary Catharine Malone and her Council Members: Sisters Martina Moynihan, Mary Ignatius Fox, Mary Stephen Durbin, Mary Joseph Ryan, and Evangelista Malone, Treasurer.

After offering congratulations to the newly-elected Mother General and her Council, Bishop Floersh went on to say to all present:

> As temporary head of this old diocese I am happy to know I have such a community as Nazareth. You are an old community now; you have existed over a hundred years and in this United States, that is almost the life of the nation... This morning I went over to your graveyard and saw there the graves of those whose names are now famous in the history of the Church in Kentucky, with whom your deceased sisters united in this great work of salvation of souls... The bishops and priests realize that without the assistance of the sisters in the schools, their arms would be shortened... And now, one word of advice. . ., I urge you to be faithful to your spiritual exercises, to be women of prayer.

Profile of the Congregation

The community that Mother Mary Catharine was elected to lead had grown in size and had become diverse in ministries during its first 112 years. It numbered 1,015 sisters in 1924. Nazareth operated three colleges; fourteen academies in Kentucky, Mississippi, Arkansas, and Maryland; sixty parochial schools in Kentucky, Mississippi, Ohio, Tennessee, Massachusetts, Arkansas, and Virginia; six hospitals in Kentucky, Arkansas, and Ohio; six orphanages in Kentucky, Virginia, Tennessee, and Massachusetts; and two homes, one for working young women in Massachusetts and one for elderly men in Kentucky.

From the time of its foundation, the character of the community had remained genuinely American with unmistakable traces of its first teachers from France, Bishop Benedict Joseph Flaget and Bishop John Baptist David. The sisters, coming as many had from rural families, remained close to the soil. They brought with them agricultural knowledge and managerial skills. By tilling the soil as their pioneer neighbors had, the sisters at the motherhouse developed a farm sizeable enough to support themselves and the student boarders.

Three members of the Durbin family of rural Meade County in Kentucky exemplified an authentic understanding of domestic management shared by many early SCNs. After holding positions of leadership in Ohio, Oregon, and Kentucky, Sister Beatrice Durbin served as Novice Mistress. Sister Joseph Leo Durbin was overseer of poultry and farm animals for fifteen years. For nineteen years, Sister Mary Stephen Durbin supervised Nazareth's farm of 1200 acres and served as a member of the Motherhouse Council before being elected to the General Council.

Sister Mary Brice McCloskey, in addition to serving as pharmacist for the motherhouse, had charge of the chickens and took pride in their fertility. She welcomed the Nazareth Academy biology classes to witness the first cracks, chirps, and emergence of the baby chicks. Sadly, in the winter of 1936, Sister Mary Brice's death resulted from a fall on the ice, as she went to make a pre-dawn check of the chicken house.

Established in 1888, Nazareth Post Office, located in Colonial Hall of the administration building, had a record of reliable handling of U.S. mail. On January 31, 1925, following the resignation of Sister Mary Joseph Ryan as Postmistress, Senator Richard P. Ernst in Washington, DC sent a telegram on January 31, 1925, to Mr. Newcome, chairman of the Republican Party in Nelson County.

The telegram read:

POSITION TO BE FILLED AT ONCE
BY ACTING POSTMASTER STOP
NOMINATE SUITABLE REPUBLICAN STOP

Mr. Newcome did not come to Nazareth himself. Instead he sent Dr. Tuttle, a well-known public figure living in Nelson County. He knew little about the SCNs or Nazareth. During his visit he observed the volume and careful handling of mail and packages passing through Nazareth Post Office. He noticed as well the good order of the entire campus. On leaving Nazareth, Dr. Tuttle said he would contact Senator Ernst in Washington who had misjudged Nazareth, supposing it to be a village in Kentucky. He talked with Sister Marie Michelle LeBray, Nazareth's nominee for the position, and was confident that one so competent would be acceptable to both Republicans and Democrats. Sister Marie Michelle's service as postmistress for the next fifteen years proved Dr. Tuttle's assessment correct.

Another activity in public life at Nazareth occurred on Election Day in 1925, when a precinct of Nelson County was established at Nazareth. Tables, surrounded by screens for voter privacy, were set up in the Academy recreation room, and voters were duly notified of the new polling place. Two years later, the annalist at Nazareth recorded:

Primary Election Day, Aug. 6, 1927. Polls open from 6 a.m. to 4 p.m. Counting of votes today not completed 'til about 6:30 p.m. The 'signing and sealing' not finished 'til 8:00 p.m. and after. Election officers: Margaret Gertrude Murphy, Judge; Mary Joseph Ryan, Clerk; Mr. C. O. Kelty, Sheriff; assisted by Mr. Victor Kelly, and Anatolia Byrne.

The arrival or departure of groups in cars was a regular occurrence at Nazareth. The Greyhound Bus extended its service by driving onto the campus to Holy Family Circle in front of the motherhouse. Exhaust fumes trailing the back of the bus marked arrivals and departures of students, sisters, and friends.

Hannah Malone

Hannah, the future Mother Mary Catharine, affectionately known as "Hannie" Malone, was born in Yazoo City, Mississippi, to Thomas and Margaret Kayes Malone on December 21, 1861, the fifth of eight children. Hannie responded to the love of parents, siblings, and playmates. Her affectionate, vivacious, and fun-loving nature became noticeable traits. When Hannie was eleven years old, she made her First Holy Communion, and at this time, unknown to anyone, she asked God to give her a religious vocation. Hannie later told relatives, "I never said anything to my father or mother about it. I was such a wild youngster, they never even dreamed I had a serious thought."

A year after Hannah's First Communion, her mother died leaving her grieving husband with eight children. Four years later, Thomas Malone followed his wife into eternity. Only then did the family learn that Elizabeth, two years older than Hannah, had also prayed for a religious vocation. The eight orphaned Malone children were not left without care. A guardian had been appointed by their father to carry out his will which provided for the education and welfare of the children until the time of their marriages. Three older brothers died young, and three sisters married.

In 1878, Elizabeth Malone, Hannah's older sister, entered the novitiate at Nazareth and received the religious name, Sister Evangelista. She endeared herself by generous and devoted service. After three years guiding Presentation Academy in Louisville, Kentucky, Sister Evangelista consecutively opened schools in Kentucky, Tennessee,

Arkansas, and an orphanage in Virginia. She served as superior at St. Catherine Academy in Lexington, Kentucky, before her final assignment as Treasurer of the Congregation from 1908 until her death on January 26, 1936.

While Sister Evangelista was in the novitiate, Hannah applied herself diligently as a student at Nazareth Academy, profiting from the broad curriculum that gave range to her creative mind. Essays in her own handwriting on varying topics reflect her interest in nature and her keen observation of people. Hannie's fun-loving personality and fondness for nature blossomed in the environment. A requirement for all pupils was the study of at least one of the fine arts. Hannie studied voice under the direction of Sister Alphonsa Kerr who had chosen religious life over a possible music career in Pittsburgh, Pennsylvania, her native city. While known for her vocal talent, the sweetness of her disposition endeared her to both students and sisters. Sister Alphonsa, teacher and mentor, and Hannah, student admirer had much in common.

Sister Mary Catharine Malone

After graduation from Nazareth Academy in June 1879, Hannah Malone entered the novitiate at Nazareth. At that time, there were 310 members and 46 novices in the congregation. On May 1, 1880, Hannah received the habit and religious name, Sister Mary Catharine. The following year she made vows. From May until August, Sister Mary Catharine again studied voice with Sister Alphonsa Kerr and was then assigned to the music department of St. Mary Academy, Paducah, Kentucky. The following year and a half she taught music in Bellaire, Ohio. Her stay was interrupted in 1885 when she received word to go to the newly-opened St. Mary's Academy in Leonardtown, Maryland. Both school and location would become synonymous with her name.

Sister Mary Catharine could best describe the surprising event that accompanied the 1885 opening of St. Mary's Academy and how she happened to become one of its founding members. The account, in her own handwriting, is preserved in the archives at Nazareth.

> On August 27, 1885 Sister Madeleine Sharkey as Superior, with Sister Rose Ann Monarch, Sister Gregorita Cotton, and Sister Bertilla Lucey arrived as the original colony at St. Mary's Academy, Leonardtown, Md. On their arrival Rev. C. K. Jenkins, S.J. asked for the music teacher. Being informed there was no music teacher among the colony, he insisted upon securing one. Nazareth was notified, and I was sent from Bellaire to take charge of the music class.

This account shows the insistence of priests for a music teacher. They wanted good liturgical music in their churches and usually depended upon the school for choirs and future organists. Local communities were glad, too, because music fees helped to meet sisters' expenses. Five years later, Sister Mary Catharine was appointed superior at St. Mary's Academy, a position she held for the next fourteen years. There she exercised an ennobling influence on generations to come.

After serving as First Assistant to Mother Alphonsa Kerr from 1904-1907, Sister Mary Catharine was appointed Mistress of Novices from 1907-1918. During those years, 400 young women entered, but only eighty-seven pronounced vows. Many of the novices returned home to help their families because of the draft of young men to the Armed Forces during World War I.

Sister Mary Catharine brought to the novitiate a wide range of gifts, optimism born of reliance on Divine Providence, prayerful resilience, and an innate spirit of joy. Handwritten notes, discovered after her death, reveal her devotion to St. Jane Frances de Chantal from whom she had gained inspiration:

> St. Jane Frances cast her seed into the ground by inspiring souls with the love of the best and the noblest, and then trusted in God's action. Gentleness and gratitude marked all her dealings with her neighbor. I have learned by experience that the best method of government is that which is sweet, humble and patient.

After a decade spent in the formation of novices, Sister Mary Catharine was elected First Assistant to Mother Rose Meagher, 1918-1924, and in July of 1924, was elected Mother General.

Mother Mary Catharine Malone

When asked to describe the newly-elected Mother Mary Catharine Malone, sisters who knew her replied: "sweet, joy-filled, kind, understanding." The theme of joy repeatedly appeared in accounts of Mother Mary Catharine's visits to the many widely-scattered SCN convents. She found happiness in nature, in friends, and in her sisters in religious life, creating or discovering joy wherever she went.

An obligation required of the Mother General during her time in office was the visitation of all SCN missions. Time was allowed for a private conversation with each sister. She also observed the work of the mission and visited with the clergy. Mother Mary Catherine was faithful to this task. According to the annals, her visitations were anticipated with joy and were a source of inspiration to the sisters.

Mother Mary Catharine did not shrink from difficult encounters regarding a host of issues, such as salaries in arrears, danger resulting from inadequate housing, and disagreements with priests. On one occasion Mother turned to the bishop for guidance. "Something is radically wrong, and I appeal to you to direct me how to deal justly and charitably in these situations." Her concern for the well-being

of the sisters led her to deal honestly and openly as seen in her letter
to Bishop J. J. Hartley of Columbus, Ohio:

> Your letter awaited me on my return from my visitation of
> our houses in Virginia and Maryland, and I am very much
> disappointed at your request to keep the sisters in Circleville.
> You say the condition is deplorable and discouraging–this is
> only a mild way of putting it, as I really do not believe anyone
> should have to live as the sisters have done during the past few
> winters.... You would have to live through it to understand.

Early in her administration Mother Mary Catharine was faced
with the death of her first assistant. A shock to the total congregation came when Sister Martina Moynihan, after a short illness, died
on March 5, 1927. The Constitutions did not explicitly direct the
procedure for selecting her replacement. Aware of her responsibility in handling this situation, Mother Mary Catharine wrote to the
Cardinal Prefect in Rome. His reply of April 15, 1927, directed the
General Council to proceed to fill the vacancy. He directed each
Council Member to move up and a new Fourth Assistant to be
elected by the Council Members. The Council General elected Sister
Dorothea Creeden as Fourth Assistant.

On July 19, 1930, the fifth General Chapter reelected Mother
Mary Catharine Malone as Mother General. Ninety-eight chapter
sisters were in attendance. Bishop John A. Floersh of Louisville presided over the elections. Mother Mary Catharine Malone's Council
consisted of: 1st assistant, Sister Ann Sebastian Sullivan; 2nd assistant,
Sister Mary John Horrell; 3rd assistant Sister Mary Stephen Durbin;
4th assistant and secretary general, Sister Bertrand Crimmins; and
treasurer, Sister Evangelista Malone.

Mother Mary Catharine was selfless as evidenced in her letter
of thanks to the sisters after the celebration of her Golden Jubilee in

1932, and in the postscript she indicates that the needs of individual sisters were important to her:

> I will use the money I received for my jubilee as a nucleus for an Education Fund for the sisters. Thus, the community that gave most of it will be the beneficiaries of it after I have passed away. I intend to add to it whatever I shall receive in the future. I think you will agree that it is a wise investment.

> P.S. I would like for Sister M. Vincena to spend four weeks in the mountains this summer. It will do her good. M.M.C.

Description of the Times

The twelve years of Mother Mary Catharine's administration coincided with years of extremes. The "roaring twenties," notable for growing prosperity, were followed by bank failures, drought, and the Great Depression. The times pointed to the beginning of a new era for the community, as it did for the nation. Changes were evident at Nazareth. The student body of Nazareth College and Academy increased. Young women came from the deep South, some remaining as resident students for three years or more until their graduation. As each prospective student entered, she brought a vista of ideas reflecting the politics and thinking of her home state. Visitors to Nazareth, clergy, parents and educators, found among the students and sisters, curious minds open to evidence of the expanding world.

Spiritual Exercises

The schedule of the day, and many of the prayers, during Mother Mary Catharine's time go back to Bishop David. His sources were St. Vincent de Paul and his own Sulpician roots. Eucharistic spirituality was central to the Congregation from its foundation. Catherine Spalding had said that once the Blessed Sacrament was reserved in a convent, she would never fear nor lose hope.

The rising bell awakened the community at 4:50 a.m. The eldest in the group said, "Benedicamus Domino" (Let us bless the Lord) to which all responded, "Deo Gratias" (Thanks be to God). In twenty minutes the community gathered in the chapel for communal prayer followed by a half-hour meditation before the beginning of Mass. Another custom among the SCNs was to spend a half-hour during the day in adoration of the Blessed Sacrament. School sisters usually attended a second Mass with students, and this sufficed for the period of adoration. Hospital sisters made their adoration as individual schedules allowed. When possible, sisters returned to the chapel before and after the noon meal for prescribed prayers. Later in the afternoon, they gathered for twenty minutes of spiritual reading. While a sister read aloud, others mended clothes or did needlework. Spiritual reading was followed by the rosary and occasional novenas. Supper, and often there was reading, was followed by a study hour for school sisters and an hour of recreation before night prayers and Sacred Silence. The sisters retired, and lights were out by 9:30 p.m.

Foreign Mission Ideas

Years before the first missionary band would leave for India, Mother Mary Catharine and Mother Rose before her, had seriously considered sending sisters to Japan, the Philippines, or to China. Motherhouse annals for November 25, 1924 read: "Father Bruno Hagspiel, SVD, renowned missionary to China, met with Mother Mary Catharine and her Council at Nazareth." Sister Mary Ignatius Fox, Secretary, wrote: "He is a man of God. He inspires others with interest in and enthusiasm for foreign mission work."

Judging from Sister Mary Ignatius' account of the meeting, it was obvious that Father Hagspiel was pressing strongly for a commitment from Mother Mary Catharine to immediate mission work in China, but she was just as strong in not committing to anything at the time. Seeing Mother's genuine interest in the missions, he continued to urge the importance of taking certain steps with which all concurred. They agreed that the time would never come when all would be ready and the community had sufficient members. Father Hagspiel emphasized working with American missionaries but not duplicating work being done by them. He advised asking the order with whom SCNs would associate to give them advanced publicity in their periodicals in order to attract missionary vocations.

Sister Mary Ignatius' notes continued:

Educational work in a mission field is very necessary. Charitable work is absolutely necessary. A combination of both is best of all. Certain financial arrangements should be clear: Who will purchase property? Who will pay for the ongoing ministry? Whatever the arrangement, it should be definite and in place for a specified time.

The age of a sister sent to foreign missions should never be above thirty-five or forty. Her character should include common sense, solid piety, love of God and love of others. Her characteristic behavior should bespeak cheerfulness. Don't send any with long faces!

Sister Mary Ignatius ended that, until the last minute, Father Hagspiel hoped that he had made a case for SCNs going to China. Though he did not get much encouragement from Mother Mary Catharine, he laughingly said goodbye to her and added, "I will pray for your conversion to missionary work in China during my Mass tomorrow morning."

Two years later, in 1926, Mother Mary Catharine wrote to Bishop Floersh asking him to obtain permission from Rome for SCNs to enter the mission field. "We feel that in the providence of

God the time has come for us to engage in missionary work in China and to accept this offering of the Passionist priests subject to your lordship's approval and that of the Holy See."

Enthusiasm for going to China gained momentum through-out the community. In a circular letter to the sisters, Mother Mary Catharine wrote: "Msgr. Dominic Langenbacher, C.P., in China is anxious that we start in September 1927. Volunteers are to apply stating age, health, parental consent, physical examination, and a health certificate from a doctor. This information is to be placed in a sealed envelope and given to the superior to send to me."

One year later, however, plans had to be changed. To Very Rev. Stanislaus Grennan, C.P., regarding the commitment to a mission in China, Mother Mary Catharine wrote: "Msgr. Dominic assured me he would not like our sisters in China until affairs become peace-able, and we hope, with God's help, to be ready for the call when it comes." When her terms of office ended in 1936, China was not yet open to missionaries, but the missionary spirit among SCNs remained alive and evident.

Renovation of the Church

After her election in 1924, the first task claiming the attention of Mother Mary Catharine and her council was the renovation of St. Vincent Church. Aware that dreams, drawings, and a significant amount of savings designated for work on the church were on hand from Mother Rose's administration, Mother Mary Catharine contacted the architect, John F. Schleblessy. She trusted in the support of her sisters, in alumnae of Nazareth Academy, and especially in Divine Providence. Mother invited the architect to meet with her and the Council members. He specified that the width and length of the church be extended by fifty feet. There would be two balconies, one above the other overlooking the body of the church, constructed on the north side connecting the convent and infirmary to the church. The sisters in the infirmary would then have easy access to the church.

A corridor on the ground level would connect the church and convent. When construction was completed, a sister teaching in the auditorium, located at the west end of the Academy, could reach the church by going through the music corridor, through the study hall, through the classrooms, through a connecting corridor to the motherhouse, down the stairway to Colonial Hall and another flight down to the ground floor, past the bell rope that called the community to prayer and into the chapel. A sister walking this route from auditorium to church would have walked 1,910 feet under one roof.

The choice of a Pilcher organ for the chapel demonstrated Nazareth's appreciation of music. The casement of quartered oak in the choir loft matched the pews below, which accommodated 860 people. The display pipes embellished in French gold bronze, numbered 138 pipes belonging to the great organ; 706 to the swell organ; 426 to the choir organ; and 204 to the pedal organ. The majestic organ enhanced worship of the faithful.

St. Vincent Church had been consecrated on July 19, 1854, by Bishop Martin J. Spalding of Louisville, Kentucky. The feast of this dedication, however, was enhanced in 1878 when Bishop William McCloskey ordained four to the priesthood in St. Vincent Church: Anthony Reinhart, Albert Murphy, Alphonse Bauer, and Charles Augustine Haeseley. He later ordained three seminarians to the diaconate in the church. Records show that all seven sacraments have been celebrated in St. Vincent Church. To SCNs, the church is a focal point for the celebration of the Eucharist, prayer, profession of vows, jubilees, funerals, and mission-sending rituals.

The towering steeples and expanding cemetery announce to anyone entering the grounds of Nazareth: "This is holy ground." The main portal to the Church with its number of receding arches and massive weathered oak doors is in harmony with the total structure. All hinge plates, door push plates, handles and bolts on the doors remind one of the strength of medieval castles. Particularly striking, they virtually cover the door inside and outside with three on each door, further complementing the vision of the architect.

During Mother Rose's twelve years in office, 1912-1924, she received gifts, large and small. These she laid aside for a purpose. She knew that soon a larger church would expand the Gothic gem built by Catherine Spalding. All the while, shaping in her mind was the vision of a pure white altar of Carrara marble. When the new church was completed, there appeared the beautiful altar of Mother Rose's vision – and of her savings.

The original color scheme of the interior emphasized the snowy whiteness of the three marble altars. A close view of the hand-carved, polished marble high altar reveals Da Vinci's Last Supper on the pediment of the altar; on the right side, The Sacrifice of Isaac; on the left side, The Sacrifice of Melchisedech. The marble altars were consecrated October 25, 1926, by Bishop John A. Floersh. Statues of the Immaculate Heart of Mary and of the Sacred Heart of Jesus, left and right of the high altar, are of unpolished Carrara marble. Originally, around the walls of the sanctuary in Gothic niches surrounding the high altar, were statues of Saints Joseph, Teresa of Avila, Catherine of Siena, Vincent de Paul, Francis de Sales, Rose de Lima, John the Evangelist, and the Virgin Mary. These statues of hand-carved teakwood were imported from Belgium.

The two side altars, graced by imported marble statues of St. Joseph and the Blessed Virgin Mary, are similar in composition and size to those of the high altar. The crown on the statue of our Blessed Mother has eight diamonds, the gift of Margaret Burke, a devoted friend who died during the flu epidemic of 1918. The communion rail of Carrara marble is ornately decorated with quatre-foils, Corinthian columns, and the Greek cross. The floor of the sanctuary is of marble mosaic.

The Stations of the Cross are oil paintings by Costaggini, an artist who assisted in painting the mural in the rotunda of the nation's capitol. Each Station was enclosed in a Gothic frame of carved oak. The discerning eye may note the smaller stature of the model used by the artist in depicting Christ in the tenth to fourteenth Stations. The Stations were a gift from the Diocese of Columbus, courtesy of Rev. Michael Meara, pastor of St. Joseph Church, Circleville, Ohio.

The stained glass windows generated a volume of correspondence between Sister Evangelista Malone, Treasurer from 1908-1936, and F. Meyer Co. of Munich and New York. Sister Evangelista was demanding and unwavering in refusing to accept a window that did not measure up to her requirements and taste. She returned a window in which the purple did not blend with the same hues in another window. She returned a second window in which the expression on a saint's face was too severe. She held out for what she thought appropriate for St. Vincent Church.

The windows are authentic Gothic in design and splendid in color. The tones of the stained glass vie with one another in mingling their polychrome tints and incandescent splendor with the subdued light of the interior of the church. Among the most beautiful windows are: The Te Deum, The Agony in the Garden, and another depicting in three parts: The Annunciation, the Nativity, and The Presentation in the Temple. The windows reveal the names of donors: alumnae, relatives of the sisters, and friends. Other benefactors remain anonymous; but their donations for the statues, organ, bells, and other accoutrements attest to their faith and loving appreciation of the sisters.

Prominent in the nave of the church are the pillars of scagliola, an ornamental marble made from chipped marble, thinly ground gypsum and Tennessee marble. The capitals are of Corinthian design. The original ceiling was beautiful to behold. The forked arches were originally of gold leaf. From the many unique gold ribs, the fan vaulting ever widening as it ascends, forms a net of gold over the blue starry sky until it reaches its zenith.

Calling the sisters to prayer are Westminster chimes, manufactured by the famous Mennely Bell Company of Troy, New York. The chimes consist of four bells made of Lake Superior copper and India tin. From these bells chime the music of Handel. The hammers are struck from lignum vitae. In 1926, each bell was inscribed with one of the characteristic virtues of the Sisters of Charity of Nazareth: humility, simplicity, charity, and zeal.

The marble whiteness of the three altars and communion railing defines the sacred space of the Eucharistic Presence. The window of The Agony in the Garden above the main altar was a gift of the Nazareth Academy alumnae. A world-traveled prelate once commented: "The beauty of this church is surpassed only by the vastness and age of some in Europe." Others named it: "The Jewel of the Archdiocese."

One might wonder how Nazareth financed this renovation in light of current and future community expenditures, some already in progress when Mother Mary Catharine took office. Minutes of Council meetings reveal that she had obtained permission from Rome to borrow $200,000 to cover the expenses of early undertakings, the renovation of the church being one among others.

Nuns of the Battlefield Monument

In 1924, a letter from Ellen Ryan, L.D., President of the Ladies Auxiliary to the Ancient Order of Hibernians of America, informed Mother Mary Catharine that Nazareth was among the congregations whose sisters, having nursed the wounded during the Civil War, were to be honored. A bronze table, entitled Nuns of the Battlefield, designed by Jerome Connor, stands on a marble pedestal to recognize the Catholic Sisters who gave their services on the battlefields and in hospitals during the Civil War. The monument clearly depicts the white cap worn by Sisters of Charity of Nazareth at that time.

The inscription on the monument reads:

They comforted the dying, nursed the wounded, carried hope to the imprisoned, gave in His name a drink of water to the thirsty.

NUNS OF THE BATTLEFIELDS WAR MEMORIAL
SCN CIVIL WAR NURSES

Alexia McKay	Mary Constantia Moran
Angela Brooks	Mary Cyril Walsh
Anita Gaitens	Mary Ida Brophy
Appolonia McGill	Mary Joseph Hollihan
Blanche Traynor	Mary Louis Hines
Borromeo McKensey	Mary Lucy Dosh
Catherine Malone	Mary Mark Byrne
Claracena Hanly	Mary Patrick McCabe
Cornelia King	Mary Peter Brady
De Chantal Kenny	Mary Sylvester Mattingly
Dominica Byrne	Mary Vincent Hardey
Erminilda Kelly	Mildred Travers
Gaudentia Beatie	Patricia Grymes
Humbaline Fagan	Philippa Pollock
Jovita Mullen	Placida Sisness
Justine Linnehan	Regina Drumm
Lauretta Maher	Scholastica Fenwick
Martha Drury	Sophia Carton
Mary Alban McGahey	Vincent Ferrer Murphy

Mother Mary Catharine informed the community of the invitation to attend the unveiling of the monument. Sister Lauretta Maher was the only living sister named on the monument. Ill health prevented her attending the ceremony, but sisters from Maryland and Virginia represented the Sisters of Charity of Nazareth on that occasion. A writer for *Time* magazine commented on the historical monument and its sculptor in this way: "Jerome Connor really made his mark most notably with this tablet." It must be noted that the War Department objected to its being erected in Arlington National Cemetery. Jerome Connor downsized the memorial and it was subsequently erected at M Street & Rhode Island Avenue, N.W. across from St. Matthew's Cathedral.

Death of Mother Rose Meagher

During Mother Mary Catharine's first term, her predecessor, Mother Rose, had been in delicate health. During her last illness, the sisters sat with Mother Rose, prayed with her, and made their final farewells. On November 2, 1930, she slipped peacefully and quietly into the welcoming embrace of God. Unable to attend the funeral of Mother Rose at Nazareth, a devoted friend of their Bellaire, Ohio days, Rev. James B. Rooney, wrote:

> This time thirty years ago we were in Bellaire together. I was just five weeks ordained. She led me by the hand to the sick and dying, to those who were out of the Church for years. Typhoid and pneumonia reaped a harvest in Bellaire. There were homes reeking in filth. Mother Rose cleaned them so that I could give the Sacraments in dignity and devotion. I walked the streets of Bellaire in tears and sorrow filled my young heart. Mother Rose was the Angel of comfort to me. The priests and people thought I worked miracles with the sick and the dying; it was dear Mother Rose who brought

them back to God. I was a child in her hand. Her personality turned many hearts back to the Church. Her deeply beautiful Catholic Faith touched the hearts of the infidel and the gambler. It was their last grace.

Educational Preparation of SCNs

When Mother Mary Catharine took office, many of the sisters on missions held diplomas from the Normal School at Nazareth. She realized that to become competent educators in the twentieth century, the sisters needed additional formal education. Mother Mary Catharine believed that no conflict existed between intellectual pursuits and the spiritual life of the sisters. At the close of Nazareth Summer School in 1925, she addressed the sisters:

> Every true Sister of Charity of Nazareth knows and acknowledges that progress in learning develops and broadens the religious spirit and makes us realize more fully what we are to God and to the Congregation... The motive behind all studies must ever be the glory of God, the good of the Order, but over and above all, our own personal sanctification.

Grateful that Sister Mary Ignatius Fox, a nationally-recognized educator, was presently on the Council at Nazareth, Mother entrusted to her the education of the sisters.

Mary Ignatius Fox, SCN

In a survey on SCN education some years later, Miriam Corcoran, SCN, wrote of the SCN stars in the field of education. She gave pride of place in her book to Sister Mary Ignatius Fox:

> A Nazareth Academy graduate of 1876, Mary Fox had been a student of Sisters Columba Carroll, Marietta Murphy, and Marie Menard, among other Nazareth educators and thus

an heir of Sister Ellen O'Connell's legacy. Mary possessed the sturdy spirit and total dedication of her foremothers to Nazareth's educational mission. Besides these assets, Mary, when she entered the novitiate in 1886, brought four years' experience as a teacher and five years as principal of St. Paul School in her native Lexington, Kentucky.

Sister Mary Ignatius began an educational career in school administration that gained her wide respect and national recognition. As director of education in the Normal School at Nazareth, Sister Mary Ignatius came full circle. She recognized limitations in educating the sisters only at the Normal School at Nazareth. She recommended that Mother Mary Catharine continue to send sisters for study at Boston College, Catholic University, Notre Dame University, Xavier University, University of Kentucky and other recognized institutions of higher learning.

In addition to formal education, experiences of the sisters were factors in their educational background. The history of the Congregation paralleled the history of the United States in its growth and development. By 1924, young women entering Nazareth as postulants came with wider experiences of travel by automobile and railway. Some came with competence to teach, others with experience in the business or the professional world. Young women influenced by the cultural and educational legacy of Sister Mary Ignatius and other sisters were now teachers in classrooms throughout the community. Their widened vision and expertise became evident in their classrooms and in the progress of their students.

Chapter Two

Academies

When Mother Mary Catharine took office in 1924, the Sisters of Charity of Nazareth had fourteen academies. With the exception of St. Mary's Academy in Maryland, all were established in the nineteenth century and located in the southern states. Mother Catherine Spalding herself opened the first four academies in Kentucky.

The goal of these schools was to give each student an education, inferior to none, augmented by sound moral and religious training. Parents were attracted to small classes and the emphasis of the curriculum on the arts, culture, and refinement. Non-Catholic parents, for these same reasons, enrolled their children, who in some academies, constituted one-third of the student body.

The Sisters of Charity of Nazareth owned the academies, and in addition to educating the students, had responsibility for the upkeep of the building and property. Furthermore, collecting tuition and school fees from parents, who often lived some distance from the school, was an ever present and sometimes difficult task.

Nazareth Academy, Nazareth, Kentucky, Est. 1814

On May 28, 1925, Nazareth Academy celebrated the 100th anniversary

SCN ACADEMIES IN KENTUCKY

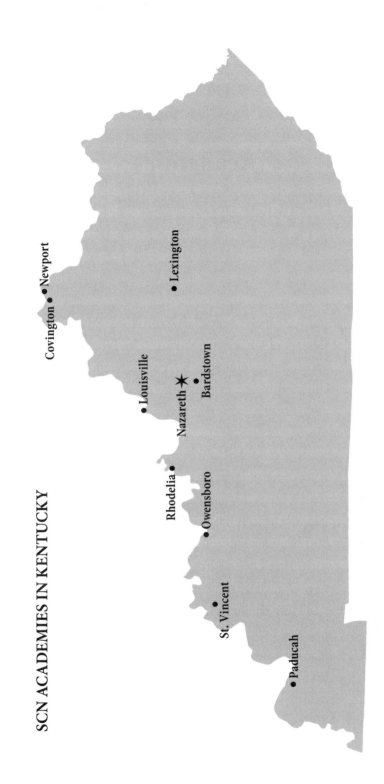

of its first commencement exercises. In covering the richness of its history, a graduate of Nazareth Academy, Carrie Turner Treacy, wrote (ca. 1929):

> The history of Nazareth is the history of Kentucky. It numbers among its patrons some of the most distinguished men of our country. Henry Clay sent his daughter, granddaughter and great-granddaughter there; Judge Benjamin Winchester, John J. Crittenden, Judge John Rowan, Zachary Taylor, Jefferson Davis, James Guthrie, George D. Prentice, Governor Charles Wickliffe, and a host of others sent their daughters or other relatives.

In 1918, Sister Mary Catharine Malone was elected first assistant to Mother Rose Meagher. She left St. Mary's Academy in Leonardtown, Maryland, where she had been superior and principal for years. In 1924, as Mother General and Head Mistress of Nazareth Academy, her interests in her alma mater widened to include the curriculum and the arts, as well as increased civic responsibility in the young nation. Mother's interest in the girls continued to foster a family relationship among sisters and students for which Nazareth became noted.

In 1924, the Nineteenth Amendment was being interpreted by many as women's emancipation from gender restrictions. The "new woman" bobbed her hair, shortened her skirt, and wore make-up. Some even smoked cigarettes. While Nazareth felt this surge of newness passing throughout the country, it held firmly to the ideals of dignity and grace.

Nazareth girls in their chapel capes and veils were a familiar sight at Mass in St. Vincent de Paul Church. The Sodality of the Blessed Virgin Mary was a popular movement to which the senior class in the Academy was invited for membership. Preceded by a day of retreat, the girls approached their entrance into the sodality with seriousness and appreciation. Classes at Nazareth and throughout the community were preceded by prayer: "O my God, I offer You this work and all my works for Your honor and glory. My Jesus, mercy! Our Lady of Divine Providence, pray for us." Many girls left Nazareth carrying with them the seeds of a lifetime devotion to Divine Providence.

The course of studies, both classical and general, kept the girls well occupied. Free time after class provided for walks on campus, horseback riding, and field sports such as hockey, golf, tennis, archery, and croquet. In addition to membership in the Catholic Students Mission Crusade (CSMC), each girl belonged to at least one specialized club such as glee club, orchestra, art, nature study, debate, and foreign language. Each Club was responsible for a monthly presentation before students and faculty.

On June 1, 1925, the Latin Club and an interested audience met at Caesar's Bridge, located within Poets' Corner near the statue of Our Lady Seat of Wisdom. Rev. Richard Davis, a native of Ireland, who served as chaplain at Nazareth for thirty-eight years, had been invited to say a few words. Discarding his notes in Latin, Father spoke instead in his Gaelic-American tongue. Then, dramatically striking the bridge with his cane, he called out something like "Caesar ego sum" as he led the group across the bridge.

A scholar of no mean accomplishments, Father Davis promoted Nazareth's academic progress and appreciation of the liturgy. A lover of literature, music, and drama, he fostered an enduring appreciation of these in teachers and students. Father Davis encouraged the girls to take advantage of the beautiful Nazareth campus, and for many years he was their golf instructor.

Bethlehem Academy, Bardstown, Kentucky, Est. 1819
The story of Bethlehem Academy holds a preeminent position among SCN schools as it was founded by Mother Catherine Spalding.

Bethlehem's first faculty was still living in the log house at St. Thomas in Nelson County even before the sisters moved the motherhouse to its present site.

In March 1929, Nazareth gave permission for the sisters to purchase the handsome old house known by residents of Bardstown as Anatok. Located across from the Academy, it would serve well as a residence for the SCN faculty. If the sisters purchased the home, immediate improvements would be needed. The *Kentucky Standard* reported that several adjoining lots to Anatok were purchased by friends of Nazareth and donated to the sisters. The final bid of $9,250 for the residence was more than Nazareth could pay. A spontaneous meeting of interested townsfolk was held on the lawn of Anatok to raise $1,000. Most gratifying about this meeting was the general enthusiasm manifested by the entire town.

The name, Anatok, given by the previous owner, is an Indian word meaning "meeting of the winds." The presence of many caves under the city gave evidence to the people of Bardstown that, in its early history, Shawnee Indians roamed the hills and forested areas covering Nelson County.

Bethlehem Academy sisters welcomed Mother Mary Catharine on her visitation in 1931. She spent the day talking with the sisters individually. On leaving that evening, Mother told the sisters that if she had time the following Saturday she would stop by to pay them a social visit, then adding in her characteristic way, "I'd like to see how nice you look when you are all together." The following Saturday, true to her word, Mother came for a friendly visit with the sisters.

Among archival materials of Bethlehem Academy were copies of a small pamphlet circulated among parishioners of St. Joseph Cathedral. The pamphlet encouraged those owing tuition to pay. "Sisters, well-trained for their work, and devoting their lives to their work, with no hope of recompense, make our schools possible. Many of the sisters' schools are on the charity list." One writer knew the people of Bardstown would not allow their school to be so listed.

During the Depression, Bethlehem's enrollment continued to grow. The student body in 1926 reached 284 students, thirty-six of whom were in high school. Aware that Immaculata Academy in Newport, Kentucky, was closing, Sister Lawrencetta Veeneman, principal of Bethlehem, asked for and received its science equipment, library books, and some chapel furnishings. At the beginning of the summer, Rev. William D. Pike presented Sister Lawrencetta with a check for one thousand dollars, the sum collected by the high school girls. The Parent Teacher Association (PTA) gave her ninety dollars raised by projects that spring.

Monday of Passion Week in April 1935 became a memorable day in the history of Bethlehem Academy. Fire, started by faulty electrical wiring, threatened total destruction of Anatok. Following the sound of the alarm, members of the fire department filled the convent lawn. Brothers from St. Joseph Preparatory School, neighbors, church-goers and older pupils gathered quickly and carried articles from the convent. Water and fire damage did serious harm to the entire building, but the rapid response to the fire by so many prevented a total loss. The Knights of Columbus offered the use of their hall for high school classes, and the PTA paid the coal bill. Nazareth never forgot the generous response of the people of Bardstown in their time of need.

St. Vincent Academy, Union County, Kentucky, Est. 1820
St. Vincent Academy, located in rural Union County, was many times referred to as a "second Nazareth." Mother Mary Catharine rejoiced with Sister Mary Celine O'Brien and sisters on learning that St. Vincent Academy received affiliation with the Catholic University of America in 1924-25. In addition, St. Vincent's became a member

of the Southern Association of Colleges and Secondary Schools, and received AA rank, the first SCN Academy to be so recognized.

In 1924, boys were admitted into St. Vincent Academy with the privilege of taking both grammar and high school courses. A "commodious bus" was purchased to transport the children of Union County to St. Vincent Academy. The number of day pupils almost doubled. In 1935, the enrollment included sixty-seven boarders, seventy-six day pupils, and twenty industrial pupils.

The classic mode of education at St. Vincent was evident in the name of the 3,000-volume library: the Aquinas School Library. Composition, creative writing, public speaking, and debate drew students into the library. St. Vincent students took an active interest in state contests where they often excelled in creative writing, art, and music. Students participated in competitive debate tournaments throughout the year. "Resolved that a farmer does more for his country than a city clerk" was a typical topic debated by pupils. Annually, the topic for debate in high schools, assigned by the moderator at Catholic Student Mission Crusade headquarters in Cincinnati, generated great interest.

St. Catherine Academy, Lexington, Kentucky, Est. 1823

Another academy opened by Mother Catherine Spalding was St. Catherine Academy on Limestone Street in Lexington, Kentucky. At one time there were twenty-seven sisters residing at St. Catherine Academy who were teaching at St. Peter School, St. Paul School, and at St. Catherine Academy.

Sister Mary Cephas Riggle, manager of the cafeteria at the Academy, charged the pupils ten cents for a hot dinner prepared by her and served by music teacher, Sister Lucille Russell or commercial teacher, Sister Alma Ruth. St. Catherine's, St. Peter's, and St. Paul's, were noted for their exceptional achievements not only in academics, but also in dramatic arts, instrumental music, and choral ensembles. The scholastic atmosphere created by sisters attending lectures at the University of Kentucky and educational conventions elsewhere had an enriching effect upon the combined faculties. Interspersed during the scholastic year were talks given by Jesuits from Chicago, St. Louis, and Cincinnati. Laywomen and men who had traveled to the Holy Land or to India showed photographic slides. The Lexington newspaper made note of these lectures and commented on the quality of their presentations. The Kentucky Classical Association sponsored Latin contests in which St. Catherine Academy students excelled both in the number of entrants and in the results.

As superior of St. Catherine's Academy in 1929, Sister Mary Dympna Francis, a capable administrator and teacher, faced an awkward situation with the Diocese of Covington. For almost a century, the original St. Peter's congregation held services in a former residence of a Catholic family. Then St. Peter's congregation built its first church on a corner lot belonging to the Sisters of Charity of Nazareth. St. Peter's congregation grew in numbers and, in 1929, a new St. Peter's Church was dedicated, three blocks away from the first one. The sisters thought the Diocese would remove the abandoned St. Peter's Church building from their lot. This, however, did not occur. The vacant church building, left locked and unused, became an eyesore in the locality. Sister Mary Dympna was notified by the City of Lexington that the tower of the church had become a safety hazard. Upon learning this, Mother Mary Catharine and her Council authorized Sister Mary Dympna to make necessary arrangements to have the building razed, and to sign the required legal contracts in the name of Nazareth Literary and Benevolent Institution.

A wrecking company from Louisville bid $500 for the work. Sister had hoped the company would accept inside materials as partial payment for their work, but the company declared the materials worthless. However, when the building was leveled, parishioners and lovers of antiques found cherished symbols of faith in the interior materials. Wood from pews, pulpit, and communion rail were readily converted into tables and picture frames. Shards of stained glass from shattered windows lived on in Catholic homes as revered icons of the faith of their fathers and mothers.

Presentation Academy, Louisville, Kentucky, Est. 1831

In 1924, when Sister Mary Anastasia Coady was principal, Presentation Academy became a member of the Southern Association of Colleges and Secondary Schools, Class A.

In 1931, Presentation Academy founded by Mother Catherine Spalding in Louisville, celebrated the hundredth anniversary of its foundation. Many expressions of praise given on that occasion added to the joy and happiness of Mother Mary Catharine and those in attendance. Msgr. G.W. Schumann shared a memory that showed the wisdom of Mother Mary Catharine.

When the former location of Presentation Academy was vacated, Mother put the property up for sale. At that time a group of Catholic men was looking for a clubhouse. Their choice fell on "Old Presentation" which they agreed to purchase for $5,000. At the end of the year, being financially embarrassed, the men could not make payment. Thinking they would have "no trouble with the gentle sisters," they wrote asking the sisters to take back the house, even suggesting the return of the down payment. In a short time, they received Mother's reply, couched in language explicitly polite, but equally firm, in its refusal of their offer. She ended it briefly: "Business is business."

In 1925, Sister Agnes Teresa McAuliffe, principal, upheld the best traditions of Presentation. To her is due the model school library, convenient and useful to both Presentation students and to library science classes at Nazareth College. The CSMC alerted many a Presentation girl and others elsewhere to an intense awareness of missionary activity and concern for people around the world. A letter from Mother Mary Catharine dated June 17, 1928, addressed to Miss Mary Burke (Mary Ransom Burke, SCN) thanked the Presentation CSMC Unit for the generous check of $500.00 for a foundation in China. Mother wrote, "The time is not yet ripe for us to embark for that foreign field, but God in His own good time will clear away all obstacles."

Activities of the CSMC enkindled religious vocations in some by awakening the desire to be part of Catholic missionary endeavors. From Presentation Academy numerous girls entered religious congregations. By 1933 this number had increased to fifty-six.

Music always played an important part in the cultural and religious life of "Pres" girls. Each student had a daily missal, and liturgies were prayed/sung congregationally in the chapel. In 1935, nine sisters from Presentation enhanced their professional preparation by participation in a two-week seminar on Gregorian Chant in New York City. Music teachers worked diligently to earn degrees at the Conservatory of Music in Cincinnati, Ohio. After teaching all week at Presentation, the music teachers took the Friday evening train to Cincinnati for music lessons on Saturday. Back in Louisville on Monday, their new knowledge became evident in their pupils' classes. The reputation of music education at Presentation Academy drew citywide attention, and its recitals/programs played to packed houses.

St. Frances Academy, Owensboro, Kentucky, Est. 1849

Nearly 75 years after SCNs began teaching at St. Frances Academy, Owensboro, the school achieved accreditation from the University of Kentucky, and the Catholic University of America. Seven years later, in 1930, the Academy was accredited by the Southern Association of Secondary Schools.

From 1926 to 1930, Sister Ann Sebastian Sullivan served as the community supervisor of schools in the Diocese of Louisville and as a valuable associate of Fr. Felix N. Pitt, diocesan school superintendent. Through her visits to the schools, Sister Ann Sebastian came to know sisters of religious orders teaching within the diocese. As principal, she enthusiastically worked with a faculty committee to select standardized testing materials for high school pupils. Father Pitt accepted her invitation to come to St. Frances, examine testing materials, observe the procedure, and hear the comments of sisters who had administered them. Father Pitt expressed his appreciation to Sister Ann Sebastian for inviting him to take part in that work in progress for the improvement of education.

The students of St. Frances ranked well in various contests in which they participated. In the first Latin tournament of the Kentucky Classical Association in 1927, Katherine Baseheart (Mary Catharine, SCN) won first prize in Virgil. In 1928, Mary Louise Berry won first prize in the state music contest. In 1929, St. Frances Academy won the prize for the best fire drill in Owensboro, and Dorothy Drury's essay on fire prevention won first prize, an honor repeated by Margaret Shea for her essay in 1931. By 1933, eighteen girls had entered the convent, and three boys, the seminary.

In September 1925, an earthquake along the New Madrid fault alarmed people of all ages. The hearts of the young of Owensboro were soothed by the uplifting music of the St. Louis Symphony Orchestra which gave a matinee performance at the Grand Theatre for children of public and parochial schools in the Owensboro area. The Knights of Columbus Dramatic Club, made up of the best talent in Owensboro, also presented "The Noble Outcast" in St. Frances Auditorium for the benefit of the Academy.

La Salette Academy, Covington, Kentucky, Est. 1856

Another SCN academy in Kentucky was La Salette Academy in Covington, named to honor Our Lady of La Salette, a hamlet near Grenoble, France. It was here that Mary was said to have appeared in 1846. Great devotion to Mary ensued and was given the Church's approval. Ten years later, the Sisters of Charity of Nazareth established La Salette Academy.

In late November 1929, the Parent Teacher Association of La Salette Academy sponsored a bazaar, card party, and dinner, hoping to net a substantial sum for the school. Much to their chagrin, electrical deficiencies marred the event. Everyone present experienced the fright and inconvenience of the power shortage. This was, however, providential because those present donated generously, and the net profit that evening enabled Sister Laurentia Gill, the superior, to correct not only the condition in the auditorium, but also to install new wiring throughout La Salette Academy.

After the visit of Mark Godman from the State Department of Accreditation, La Salette received word that the library must be renovated. During the summer, under the direction of Sisters Augustine Porter and Mary Celine O'Brien, about 2000 volumes were classified and catalogued. Workmen with saws and hammers created much dust and noise as they set about dismantling and remaking shelves. Intent on classifying the 2,000 books, Sisters Augustine and Mary Celine seemed to ignore the whirr of the saw and the sting of the grit in their eyes. The librarian of the Covington Public Library offered valuable suggestions and helped type the Library of Congress cards. Distinctive book plates designed by Sister Anna de Paul Johnson were made for the La Salette Academy library. Additions such as *Encyclopedia Americana, Warner's World's Best Literature*, a Latin dictionary, a classical dictionary, and Garnett Gosse's *History of English Literature* were welcome contributions.

The 75th Jubilee celebration of the school began on June 13, 1931, with class night exercises. The alumnae joined in a grand chorus singing the hymn to Our Lady of La Salette composed years before by Sister Angela Strain. Many letters of gratitude and fond memories from former faculty members and alumnae were read.

In September 1930, La Salette Academy applied for affiliation with the Southern Association of Secondary Schools and in December received word that the state had approved the school. At a subsequent meeting in Atlanta, however, the school was nearly rejected because so many of the pupils were carrying five subjects. Sister Mary Ignatius Fox, Dean of Nazareth College, Nazareth, was present and explained that the fifth subject was usually music or art. In addition, the Association gave La Salette an extension to have a trained librarian on the faculty.

In December 1931, an article in the newspaper announced that work was to start immediately on a $135,000 addition to La Salette Academy. The new two-story brick and stone structure would house eleven classrooms for high school classes, twelve music rooms, a library, and an auditorium with a seating capacity of five hundred. All associated with LaSalette rejoiced in anticipation of the new building.

Immaculata Academy, Newport, Kentucky, Est. 1857

In 1925, the future of Immaculata Academy in Newport looked bright. Admission of twenty-eight boys for the second year seemed to point to renewed growth. In order to offer a commercial program to interested students, Mother Mary Catharine appointed another sister to the faculty. Additional classrooms, including a science laboratory, were provided by sacrificing a hallway. In that year, of all schools affiliated with Catholic University, members of the junior and sophomore classes of Immaculata Academy received the highest averages on test scores in chemistry. In Class A basketball, the boys won a trophy. Located in the poorest section of Newport, it was not surprising that by 1927, the enrollment at Immaculata Academy had declined. The opening of a new parish school in adjacent Southgate drew some families away, and others moved to areas of Cincinnati, Ohio.

With the deep regret of loyal alumni, parents and students, in June 1932, Immaculata Academy was closed at the end of its seventy-fifth year. The breadth of sadness was reflected in Mother Mary Catharine's letter:

> In no other institution under our guidance has the spirit of cooperation and loyalty to the sisters been more marked. Those who have labored among you the past seventy-five years have experienced it; those who have not been so favored have heard of it.

St. Mary Academy, Paducah, Kentucky, Est. 1858

Ranked among Nazareth's eldest daughters, another Kentucky academy, St. Mary Academy, Paducah, dated from 1858. The school survived the tumultuous years of the Civil War.

A graduate of St. Mary Academy, Pat Lalley, at his annual St. Patrick's Day party, never failed to offer a toast to the Sisters of Charity of Nazareth for their contribution to Catholicity in the Paducah area. Pat credited the sisters for their part in evangelizing western Kentucky. One major evangelization method, used by the sisters, was children's dramatizations of the Bible passages read on Sundays by foreign-born priests not yet fluent in the English language. These dramatizations of the gospel reached beyond the school into the homes, where parents and other relatives absorbed the gospel message.

The *News Democrat*, one of Paducah's daily papers, on receiving an issue of the school paper wrote:

Life and Ministry

A copy of the March issue (1925) of The Mignonette, a monthly journal published by the students of St. Mary's Academy, is a most creditable paper, attractive both in its form and material. It reveals throughout careful editing and good taste.

The first community service pins awarded to any Paducah Girl Scouts went to St. Mary's Troop 2. The distinguished scouts were Nell Puryear (later Mary Ellen Puryear, SCN) and Velma Roof (later Linus Mary Roof, SCN). Each had given 150 hours of community service to earn this award.

Dismissal at the close of the school day at St. Mary Academy was a spectacle in itself, not overlooked by citizens of Paducah. The principal standing on the top step, clapping the beat, and calling "Left, Right," signaled to the student pianist to begin playing March Militaire for dismissal. A sister at the foot of the steps nodded as the marchers made a square turn and continued to march in silence to the corner where, before and after school, St. Mary Academy Boy Scouts served on safety patrol.

The trend in education to include more science classes in the curriculum was reflected in 1931 with the decision to renovate the art room to accommodate chemistry classes. The Parent Teacher Association assumed the expense of equipping the science room. Two years later, Mother Mary Catharine approved further construction to accommodate the growing school. As enrollment increased, so did music pupils, and two floors of a special wing were allocated to the music department. In addition to giving private lessons, five music teachers were kept busy with orchestra, band, and glee club.

The CSMC Unit at St. Mary's sent strong representatives in debate and oratory to higher levels of competition. The crusaders were energized when Rev. Daniel A. Lord, S.J., spoke in St. Francis de Sales Church on "What Jesuits Have Undergone in North America."

His description of the North American martyrs inspired and challenged the students.

On October 15, 1933, Mass at St. Francis de Sales was offered in thanksgiving for the blessings that had come to the parish through St. Mary Academy during the seventy-five years of SCN ministry in Paducah. At that time, the student body numbered 426.

St. Theresa Academy, Rhodelia, Kentucky, Est. 1870

When Mother Mary Catharine was elected in 1924, maintenance of St. Theresa Academy in rural Rhodelia, a school for girls in Meade County since 1870, presented a problem. Income to maintain the facility was chiefly dependent upon boarders who were fewer in number each year. With regret, Sister Theolinda Bowling, superior, wrote a letter to parents notifying them and the general public that, as of November 1926, no more boarders would be accepted at St. Theresa Academy. With an enrollment of fifty-one, St. Theresa's continued as a parochial day school for both boys and girls.

Mother Mary Catharine and her Council advised Bishop Floersh of the need for extensive repairs that included updates in light, heat, and water services at the school and asked for diocesan assistance to address the situation. No assistance was forthcoming and, in 1931, Mother Mary Catharine asked Bishop Floersh for permission to withdraw the sisters from Rhodelia. This request was denied. With characteristic, but later questionable obedience, the sisters combined thrift and hard work, fortitude and prayer, and continued to educate the children of Rhodelia.

In 1932, St. Theresa School became a Meade County public school, and the board of education agreed to pay the salary of one degreed teacher. The salary received by that sister equaled the amount paid by the sisters for their farm manager. With help from Nazareth and dependence upon Divine Providence, SCNs remained true to their history of education to the poor.

News that a highway would someday pass the church, school, and convent, was kept alive by landowners and dreamers. Travel to and from Nazareth via Louisville continued to be mainly on the Ohio River. In 1932, for example, the steamer Southland left Louisville at 2 p.m. and arrived about 9 a.m. at St. Teresa Landing bringing Sister Ann Sebastian, diocesan supervisor. Traveling with her were two companions who would spend the summer in Rhodelia, a favorite vacation site for some SCNs. The water in the historic St. Patrick's spring was very refreshing throughout the summer, and sisters who liked to gather wild flowers, ferns, and moss found Rhodelia a mecca. Teams of SCNs taught religious education classes in nearby Paynesville and Andyville. Other sisters could arrange to visit their families in the area.

St. Clara Academy, Yazoo City, Mississippi, Est. 1892
For some weeks prior to November 3, 1926, the sisters at St. Clara Academy, Yazoo City, Mississippi had been eagerly anticipating Mother Mary Catharine's homecoming. This was her first visit home since leaving Yazoo City forty-six years before. Relatives and friends paid frequent visits to St. Clara's to see her. She greeted many visitors and delighted Yazoo City by recalling names and faces of two generations. Her brother, Patrick, and family came from Greenwood, Mississippi.

During October 1927, the high school supervisor visited St. Clara. He told the principal, Sister Anastasia Rice, that the eight grades of the school would remain on the probationary list. Signs of approaching hard times cautioned against incurring expenses for needed corrections. Sister Anastasia knew that in order to save the school, she must make some improvements. During the Christmas vacation, she had two windows installed in the study hall to improve

SCN ACADEMY IN MISSISSIPPI

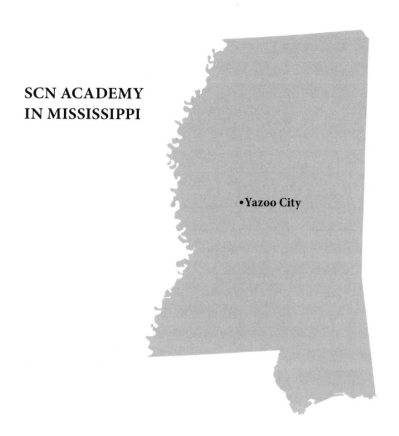

•Yazoo City

lighting. The next summer she had classroom windows enlarged. A chemistry laboratory was provided by partitioning a part of the primary classroom. To provide an additional classroom, a movable partition was placed in the study hall. These improvements saved St. Clara Academy.

In January 1934, St. Clara Academy girls played their first basketball game with the Hilltoppers of St. Joseph Academy in Natchez. "Both showed good pass work but the final whistle showed the Hilltoppers the victors." Entries in the annals, from this point on, reflect growing interest and participation in athletics. That same year the enrollment was 132.

Sister Emerentia Wales, who lived at St. Clara Academy for forty years, was often asked to tell her favorite story. Sister remembered well that when she was Eliza, a little girl in Louisville, Kentucky, her mother often took her for afternoon walks along the river front. They frequently saw Mother Catherine Spalding returning from the wharf. Mother Catherine was often carrying a baby in her arms with a little girl or boy clutching her skirts. Eliza's mother whispered "That sister will someday be a saint of the Church." At Sister Emerentia's death in 1937, her many friends and pupils eulogized her life in the local press. The headline for an editorial in the Yazoo City newspaper stated: "Last Living Link with Foundress Dies."

Annunciation Academy, Pine Bluff, Arkansas, Est. 1880

The celebration of the Golden Anniversary of Annunciation Academy in 1930 was to give appropriate recognition and honor to the Sisters of Charity of Nazareth. The Sisters had continued to build on the school's solid foundation since 1880 and brought the school to a high level of excellence.

Throughout their administrations as superiors and principals, Sisters Mary Realino Ryan (1923-1929) and Mary Constance Rapp (1929-1935) looked first to maintaining the academic standards of the school. Music teachers, instrumental and vocal, maintained the high quality of their department. Teachers in the traditional academic areas, including kindergarten, were also making notable progress.

Clippings from articles in the Pine Bluff newspaper, *The Commercial*, reporting the Golden Jubilee revealed the quality of education Annunciation Academy provided:

> When a school produces either a writer of music, song or story, it boasts of the honor, but when one of its students possesses the three talents, it may well be proud. Such an honor goes to Annunciation Academy. . . through Bessie Altheimer, Class of '29, composer of many songs, writer of verse and author of a drama.

SCN ACADEMIES IN ARKANSAS

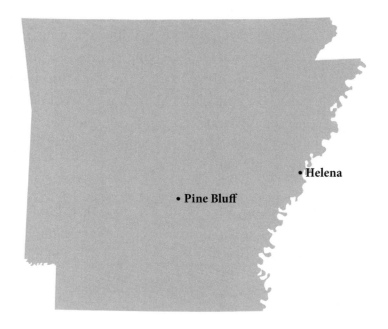

The standards of education at Annunciation Academy and its teacher preparedness were exemplary. For example, before opening the kindergarten, Miss Ione Williams was sent to visit some of the best kindergartens in St. Louis, Memphis, and Omaha. Miss Williams spent six weeks at the Normal School at Nazareth, Kentucky, where she took intensive training under leading instructors to learn how a kindergarten should be operated.

Sacred Heart Academy, Helena, Arkansas, Est. 1878

Sacred Heart Academy in Helena, Arkansas, was one of the most beautiful SCN academies, but it needed funds. Sister Ursula Palmer and members of the Expression Class staged a clever program entitled "All About Helena." The purpose was to raise funds by advertising the various businesses in Helena. The undertaking raised funds to buy some school equipment. This success encouraged other efforts to raise money for small improvements at the Academy. These endeavors could not match the more urgent need for upkeep and repair of the deteriorating building. In 1927, Mother Mary Catharine advised the local superior, Sister Mary Loretto Carroll, to ask Bishop John B. Morris of Little Rock for assistance in this expense, reminding him that for forty-eight years the Sisters of Charity of Nazareth had provided education in Helena with no remuneration from the parish or diocese. Conversation regarding cost of repairs remained at a discussion level only.

And so, another question arose and remained unaddressed by parochial or diocesan voices: Should Sacred Heart Academy become a parochial school, or should it be closed? This question remained unanswered. With characteristic fidelity to the needs of the children and with support from Nazareth, the sisters continued to provide quality education and care of the pupils attending Sacred Heart Academy. All rejoiced with the faculty when, in 1931, Sacred Heart Academy gained accreditation by the Department of Education in Arkansas.

The purchase of a grand piano for Sacred Heart Academy showed the importance placed upon music. The piano was on the stage when a school recital honored Mother Mary Catharine's visitation in May 1927. Music pupils at Sacred Heart Academy repeatedly ranked high in district and state competition.

An outreach in missionary endeavor began in Helena in 1929 when Sisters Mary Auxilium Minton and Teresa Carmel Whittinghill were appointed to teach religious education at St. Cyprian's, a parish for the African American community of Helena. Sister Teresa Carmel, a music teacher, soon had the parish singing some Gregorian chant. Sister Mary Auxilium involved pupils in class work and learning projects that made the Sunday session enjoyable.

Never had Sacred Heart Academy looked lovelier than on Mother Mary Catharine's final visit. Her companion, Sister Bertrand Crimmins, seeing the Academy for the first time, noted the beauty of the well-kept grounds, the magnificent magnolias and graceful crepe myrtle, the variety of flowers and plants. Charmed by this loveliness, Sister Bertrand exclaimed, "I would rank the campus of Sacred Heart Academy second only to that of Nazareth!"

SCN ACADEMY IN MARYLAND

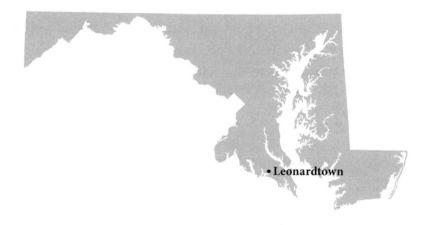

• Leonardtown

St. Mary's Academy, Leonardtown, Maryland, Est. 1885

Nineteen years of Mother Mary Catharine's early apostolate at St. Mary's Academy in Leonardtown identified her as an efficient administrator and superior with a heart. The sisters living and teaching at St. Mary's made the school "homey" and a happy place that would live in treasured memories of the students. Sister Berenice Greenwell, who knew Mother Mary Catharine very well, said that each child at St. Mary's Academy received careful attention. Mother Mary Catharine made herself accessible to students for a friendly talk, for guidance, in fact, for anything that would be helpful to the individual. Her manner of relating carried over to the faculty who shared a common goal – to give the girls at St. Mary's principles that would help them develop into mature Christian women.

On March 25, 1936, fifty years after the first Sisters of Charity of Nazareth had arrived in Maryland, Lawrence J. Kelly, S. J., spoke at the blessing of a cornerstone of the new St. Mary's Academy in Leonardtown. He reminded the crowd that fifty years before, five or six other teaching orders had been invited to break ground in Maryland but had declined. He continued saying, that Nazareth Superiors may have reasoned something like this:

> In the distant past, Maryland sent some of her best citizens – her best and bravest blood – to Kentucky and peopled what was then a wilderness. Should we SCNs not make some return to Maryland? And so today – fifty years later – is it not reasonable to think that Nazareth Superiors, recognizing that the Church in Kentucky had been carried across the Alleghenies by farming families of Catholic Maryland – thought it time to share with the Church in Maryland opportunities for education? We salute and thank the many Sisters of Charity of Nazareth who for fifty years at St. Mary's Academy and other elementary schools have lived among us and taught by word and example the Christian life.

On that same day Rev. John F. Fenlon, Superior General of the Sulpicians in the United States, unknown to the Sisters at St. Mary's Academy, happened to be in Washington, D.C. Most Rev. John McNamara, who was scheduled to bless the cornerstone of the new St. Mary's, prepared to journey from Baltimore to Leonardtown. Presuming that the Sulpician Superior would also attend, Bishop McNamara arranged that they travel together. The sisters, unaware that Father Fenlon was in the United States, had not invited him. Upon the arrival of the clergy, to the embarrassment of the sisters, this oversight became evident. Father Fenlon gently chided the sisters saying that they had slighted the Sulpician Order of which their founder, Bishop John Baptist David, and their first bishop, Bishop Benedict Joseph Flaget, were members.

The narrator of this story said that the sisters could not remain embarrassed long in the presence of so genial a personality as Father Fenlon. Conscious that more SCNs had gathered in the community room to hear every detail of his account of the Sulpician-Charity connection, Father Fenlon talked at length with them and answered their questions. The sisters felt drawn to him almost as if he were Bishop David himself; and, upon his departure, the sisters realized his presence and sharing were blessings they would always prize.

In May 1936, Father Louis C. Vaeth, S.J. called a meeting of directors of the CSMC units in Southern Maryland to plan for a Pontifical Field Mass demonstrating the strength of Catholicity there. He turned to the principal of St. Mary's Academy, Sister Mary Aline Kearns, to oversee details. He asked her to communicate with principals of participating schools regarding arrival, positioning, and dismissal of the pupils in an orderly manner. Having heard the singing in SCN schools, Father Vaeth knew that, under SCN direction, the merged choirs at the Field Mass would recreate the beauty and solemnity of the Gregorian chant. His closing remark was, "I know your sisters will remind the children to wear their best uniforms as they will process behind their school banners."

The SCN academies provided a well rounded education for girls and, in some instances, boys. Through the years, the alumni of these schools remained loyal to their alma mater. This, in itself, gives testimony to the affection for and appreciation of SCN academies by those who attended them. The dedication of the sisters not only to educational endeavors but to the very lives of their students was not forgotten by former graduates. In the case of boarders, often far from home and family, the sisters gave twenty-four hour care. Many of those who received this deep concern for their welfare remembered it forever. The history of the SCN community is, in part, intertwined with it academies.

Influences on Catholic Education

Catholic Students Mission Crusade

No account of Catholic Education in the United States is complete without special mention of the Catholic Students Mission Crusade. Founded in 1918, the primary aim of this federation, according to *The Catholic Encyclopedia*, was to acquaint Catholic students with the problems and goals of the missionary church in the United States and in other countries. Especially active in high schools and colleges, the CSMC offered opportunities for enriching the curriculum through debate, oratorical contests, essays, plays, study of and sacrifice for home and foreign missions. In addition, it afforded opportunities for leadership and rallies that brought together CSMC units from numerous schools.

Ongoing growth in mission endeavors among CSMC moderators included copying articles for the blind. Mission club moderator at St. Vincent Academy, Sister Victoria Shea, copied *The Soul of Ireland*, a book in Braille. Sister Mary Madeleine McMahon, also at St. Vincent Academy, completed *To the Dark Tower*, a 500 page book in Braille. The manuscripts in Braille type were sent to New York City to the Xavier Free Publication Society for the Blind directed by Rev. J. Stodelman, S.J. For this work, each sister received a trophy of recognition from the International Federation of Catholic Alumnae.

International Federation of Catholic Alumnae (IFCA)

The IFCA was founded in 1914 in Emmitsburg, Maryland for the purpose of coordinating the various Catholic Alumnae Associations throughout the country. Its goal was to disseminate literature, advocate continuing education, promote social services, and assist each respective alma mater. Sisters of Charity of Nazareth attended the IFCA conferences along with alumnae from SCN schools. Mother Mary Catharine, in her letter of September 10, 1924, wrote: "There will be one sister from Nazareth, Sister Mary Ignatius Fox, to attend the IFCA; from Presentation, Sister Mary Anastasia Coady; from Nazareth College, Sister Teresa Clare Goode; from St. Vincent's Academy, Sister Joseph Mary McDonough; from Hyde Park, Sister Anna Louise Mattingly." Such a commitment by the Mother General showed the importance placed upon the IFCA.

On November 14, 1925, the Kentucky Chapter of the IFCA held its annual meeting in Owensboro, Kentucky. Speaker, Katie Driscoll of Louisville said, in part: "We have now over 500 alumnae groups in 41 states... Who were the early educators of our state? The sisters and clergy and these received their education from early missionaries. Does it not seem loyal now for us to help in the field of education?" Katie Driscoll continued her address by stressing the study of Church History, its cultural background, Church Art, Gregorian Music, and reading to stay abreast of the times.

Chapter Three

The Story of
Three Colleges

I t was not until the 20th century that the SCN community ventured into higher education by establishing three colleges. All were based in Kentucky and in close proximity to each other. Two were located in Louisville, and the third was near Bardstown. The earliest, St. Helena Commercial College, was opened in response to the educational needs of young men and women preparing for employment.

Only a year separated the opening of Nazareth College, Louisville, a four-year liberal arts college, and Nazareth Junior College, on the motherhouse campus. During Mother Mary Catharine's term in office, all three colleges, because of the dedication and sacrifices of the sisters and lay faculty, continued to develop and grow. These Kentucky institutions established a reputation for excellence that spread beyond the state.

St. Helena's Commercial College, Louisville, Kentucky
Although bearing the title "college," St. Helena's was in reality a standard commercial school. It came into existence in 1913 at the request of a group of young people with employment as their goal.

It developed into a first class commercial school conducted by the Sisters of Charity of Nazareth. St. Helena's graduates "made good." Excerpts from letters of the 1920s attest to the competence of these graduates:

> It has been a pleasure to have had several of your students in our office. At present we have two St. Helena graduates. Sound moral training and high average of scholarship are characteristic of your graduates. (C. I. & L. Railway)

> We find that the young ladies in our employ from your school... have been trained to consider their obligations and duties in the commercial world, to faithfully perform what is assigned to them, and to seek the tasks which advance the work of the office. Each of these ladies is competent, painstaking, energetic and praiseworthy. (United Mercantile Agencies)

Such praise for St. Helena Commercial College graduates was due in part to the traditional curriculum in preparation for employment: shorthand, typing, bookkeeping, and office practice. In addition, the faculty offered a classical course of study in Latin, Spanish, English, civics, mathematics, and science. For their spiritual development, students had retreats, religion classes, and CSMC membership. This was balanced by athletics and regular social activities planned by the faculty and students.

The early history of St. Helena's records that in 1916, St. Helena's Cooperative Club was founded. It was organized by Father Charles P. Raffo, Sister Constance Davis, and eleven young women from the school. The purpose of the club was to engage club members in social, cultural, and charitable projects. For many years, the club furnished bandages for a leper colony in India. In gratitude, a village church in India was named St. Helena.

During World War I, club members sewed and knitted for the soldiers at Camp Taylor in Kentucky. They also worked to provide scholarships for needy students. The numerous charitable works of club members spanned the early part of the twentieth century. Many, however, would say that their most important work was the founding of St. Helena Night School to make available completion of a high school education. Though the students were nominally in charge, they depended greatly upon the sisters for direction, staffing, and maintenance of the school.

Mother Mary Catharine visited St. Helena's on October 10, 1928. She congratulated the young women for their zeal and enterprising spirit in initiating the night high school. Some of the students were veterans of World War I; others, because of economic conditions had not completed high school. The young women who opened the night school had no experience in operating a school. In 1932, Depression realities and the inability of most students to pay tuition forced the club to turn for help to Sister Mary Canisius Wilson, superior at St. Helena's. With confidence in the value of the night school, and in the tradition of "sisters helping sisters," Sister Mary Canisius and faculty arranged to use nearby Presentation Academy's chemistry laboratory for classes.

Two Nazareth Colleges

When Mother Mary Catharine was elected, the two colleges, both named Nazareth, were approximately forty miles apart. The Louisville campus was often referred to as "Nazareth College in the City." The motherhouse campus was called "Nazareth College, Nazareth." On occasions they shared faculties and resources, but remained separate entities.

Nazareth College, Louisville

On October 4, 1920, the SCN community had opened Nazareth College in Louisville during the term of office of Mother Rose Meagher. Initially, Mother Rose was named president of the young college located in the heart of the city. Nazareth College was the first four-year liberal arts institution for women in the Commonwealth of Kentucky.

The year 1924 was a banner year for the fledgling college. The first six graduates received bachelor degrees; Sister Mary Eunice Rasin offered a class in journalism and inaugurated *The Pelican*, the first student publication; and the Nazareth College Alumnae Association came into being. In 1927, the Nazareth College Guild was organized and began its many generous efforts to support the young college by card parties, bazaars, and other fund-raising activities. This guild gave years of dedicated support to Nazareth College.

There were many efforts on the part of the College to offer educational, cultural, and religious opportunities to the citizens of Louisville. Nazareth College provided lectures, book reviews, musical programs and dramas for the public. The College also sponsored retreats and days of prayer.

In October 1924, an address given to members of the CSMC sparked the students' interest in rural vacation Bible schools. The following summer, six Nazareth College students volunteered as catechists at Wax and Dog Creek near Leitchfield, and at Sunfish, Kentucky. Despite primitive conditions, seven additional college women volunteered the following summer.

Political activism was evident during the presidential campaign of 1928 between Catholic Democrat, Al Smith, and Protestant Republican, Herbert Hoover. When the sisters tried to cast their votes in the election, they were pushed and shoved, experiencing the anti-Catholic prejudice rampant at the time. Undeterred by such bigotry, they remained staunch supporters of Al Smith.

Sister Berenice Greenwell, Dean of Nazareth College, Louisville (1924-1932), established an informal curriculum based on private tutorials, granted approval by the Catholic University of America. In 1929, the sisters provided graduate work in library science, primarily for school librarians. These courses were the first of their kind in Kentucky. Sister Mary Canisius pioneered this effort and continued her ministry in library science for more than twenty-five years. During the tenure of Sister Berenice Greenwell (1924-1932), the enrollment at Nazareth College grew slowly but steadily, and by the mid-thirties, the college had graduated over 300 women.

The first efforts of the congregation toward offering courses in nursing education outside a hospital setting, occurred at Nazareth College in Louisville in the summer of 1933. Miss Honor Murphy (Nazareth Academy 1911) taught the initial group of twenty-eight students from nine Louisville hospitals.

Sister Miriam Corcoran in *A Survey of the Educational Ministry of the Sisters of Charity of Nazareth* (1996) quotes an early student:

> There is an ever-present spirit that has permeated Nazareth College for twenty-five years...the spirit of self-sacrifice. It was the complete unselfishness of courageous women who gave us our College. The real essence of the school was the firm, strong, compelling personalities of the sisters who founded and carried on the College and who made so much out of so little.

During Mother Mary Catharine's administration, faculty members at the two colleges distinguished themselves through scholarly research and writing. Sister Mary Adeline Scanlon's 1925 findings about the origin of glycuronic acid were cited in the 1927 *Proceedings of the Society for Experimental Biology and Medicine.*

Sister Columba Fox wrote *The Life of Bishop J. B. M. David* for her master's thesis while at the Catholic University of America. It was published in 1925 by the United States Catholic Historical Society. In 1930, Sister Margaret Gertrude Murphy's dissertation, *St. Basil and Monasticism*, was accepted at the Catholic University of America as partial fulfillment for her doctorate. Also in 1930, Sister Mary Eunice Rasin's dissertation for her doctorate in English at Notre Dame University, *Evidence of Romanticism in the Poetry of Medieval England*, was published. In 1935, Sister Mary Emily Keenan, wrote her dissertation, *The Life and Times of St. Augustine as Revealed in His Letters* for her doctorate at the Catholic University of America. In 1936, Sister Mary Ramona Mattingly's dissertation, *The Catholic Church on the Kentucky Frontier: 1785-1812* was published. Her doctorate in history at the Catholic University of America became a major resource for early Kentucky Catholic history. Since that time, many other SCNs have written books and articles, but the above were among the first in the arena of scholarly publications.

Nazareth College, Nazareth, Kentucky

In September 1921, while continuing as head of Nazareth Academy, Sister Mary Ignatius Fox directed the opening of Nazareth Junior College on Nazareth campus. Although the college emphasized teacher training, classes in the liberal arts were also available. In January 1922, Nazareth College, Nazareth, Kentucky, received accreditation from the Kentucky Department of Education and was able to confer teachers' certificates. In its beginning, Nazareth College, Nazareth, benefited from the keenness of the educational insights and experience of Sister Mary Ignatius. She identified sisters for future study in the fields in which they were teaching. As administrator of the schools at Nazareth, one of her valuable achievements was requesting and receiving retroactive recognition of certification for sisters who had successfully completed work in the Normal School at Nazareth. She also inaugurated adjustments necessary for the Normal School to receive accreditation by the Kentucky Department of Education. In 1929, Nazareth Junior College gained admission to the Southern Association of Colleges and Schools.

Sister Mary Ignatius introduced a broad educational program for the summer schools at Nazareth. The diocesan paper of Louisville, *The Record*, described the 1925 summer school:

At the sound of the eight o'clock bell Monday morning, June 22, the student body filled the Assembly Hall. At a signal from Sister Mary Ignatius Fox, they dispersed to the various classrooms, where a distinguished faculty included:

Rev. Leo Keaveney, Ph.D., Supervisor of Schools,
    St. Cloud, Minnesota, Professor of Education;
A.L.Witherspoon, Ph.D. of Yale University,
    Professor of English;
C.H. Howard, Ph.D. of Catholic University,
    Professor of Philosophy;
Señor Maya, A.B., B.S. of the University of Madrid,
    Professor of Spanish;
Mr. B. F. Hasty of the Louisville Normal School,
    Teacherof Primary Methods;
Miss Carolyn Strubel, Supervisor of Physical
    Education in the Louisville Public Schools,
    Professor of Physical Education.

Added to the illustrious list were several distinguished SCN professors. At the same time the summer school was in session for classroom teachers, the music teachers also had some of the best professors available. Such a brilliant assembly recalls the visiting lecturers from neighboring St. Joseph College and St. Thomas

Seminary invited to Nazareth Academy by Bishop David and Sister Ellen O'Connell.

A gymnasium had long been a dream at Nazareth. In 1929, at the ground-breaking, Father Davis declared, "The school is growing as I have never before seen it grow. Soon we will have an athletic department which has long been needed. You girls will no longer have to resort to pillow fights for exercise."

Nazareth accomplished a major goal with the construction of a modern gymnasium. The alumnae, who generously supported the building fund, insisted that it be named "Ignatius Hall." At the dedication, Ben Johnson, former Congressman, spoke of the growth and importance of Nazareth College, asserting, "Its influence is felt from the Atlantic to the Pacific."

Sallie Britton, daughter of the mayor of St. Louis, Missouri attended Nazareth Academy (1864-1866). Later, as Countess Spottiswood-Mackin, she left a sizeable amount to Nazareth in her will. In a letter of appreciation to her lawyer, Mother Mary Catharine wrote:

> The Princess remained honorary president of our Alumnae Association to the time of her death. The Alumnae Yearbook for 1923 shows her picture with that title underneath.... Our Alumnae Association has recently erected for us at Nazareth a very fine gymnasium on which there is considerable debt. I think it would please Princess Spottiswood-Mackin to have her name inscribed on the bronze tablet placed in this handsome building to commemorate the donors, so the gift will be placed to that account.

Performances that the young women gave for their parents, the sisters and visitors were an unforgettable aspect of Nazareth College. The students were generous with their time and talent. The debates, dramas, dance programs, musical recitals, and athletic contests were not only educational for the students, but brought culture and entertainment to audiences in general. These events, in addition to the academic offerings, helped to enhance the college's reputation.

For Nazareth's three colleges, the spirit of service stands out as a vital part of the educational process. The students demonstrated this spirit in the multitude of activities in which they engaged to help others, especially those in need. In a letter to college students, Mother Mary Catharine wrote: "You cannot rest with merely receiving the rich inheritance of your college education, but will increase your share by living a life impelled by the love of Christ."

SCN EDUCATION IN KENTUCKY

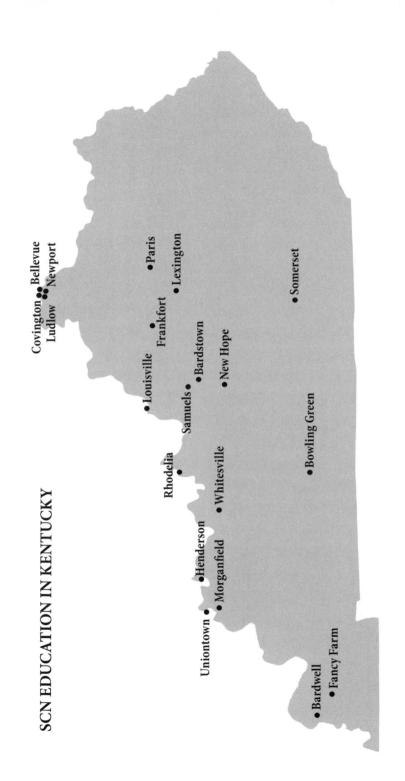

Covington • Bellevue
Ludlow • Newport

Paris •
Lexington •

Frankfort •

Somerset •

Bardstown •
Louisville • New Hope •

Samuels •

Rhodelia •

Whitesville •

Bowling Green •

Henderson •
Morganfield •

Uniontown •

Bardwell • Fancy Farm •

Chapter Four

Education in Kentucky
1924-1936

"The parish school is the church's distinct contribution
to American citizenship. It is the very cornerstone of
Catholicism in our country."

—Rev. Joseph A. Dunney

*D*uring Mother Mary Catharine's time in office, SCNs,
assisted by a small number of lay teachers, staffed thirty-four
"cornerstones of Catholicism" in Kentucky and taught in
three of the state's public schools, as well. This chapter describes
various aspects of each of these schools.

In addition to providing historical details from archival records,
the chapter draws on the SCN tradition of storytelling. The stories
come not only from anecdotal entries of the annalists, but also from
living SCNs who remember those days. Somewhat comparable
to photos in a snapshot album, they create a sense of the times as
experienced in the daily operations of these schools and in the lives
of all involved with them.

Against a backdrop of repeated references to economic difficulties,

---

*Dunney, Joseph A. *The Parish School: Its Aims, Procedures, and Problems.* New York: Macmillan, 1921.

the stories focus on dedicated teachers, high student achievement, support of parents, parishioners, clergy, and civic-minded individuals whose universal willingness to sacrifice would suggest that these parochial schools survived and flourished with no aid other than that of the people who loved them.

Most of Mother Mary Catharine's term paralleled the "boom to bust" period of the early 20th century. The Great Depression, when it arrived, showed no favorites. As can be seen in problems faced by urban schools within the diocese, hardship did not stop at the city limits. Still, Mary Mother Catharine had a penchant for children in rural areas where education was often hampered by lack of passable roads and bridges. It was not uncommon for rural children to miss classes in order to help with planting and harvesting. Despite such circumstances, and in spite of small enrollments that seldom reached a hundred, Mother Mary Catharine remained dedicated to rural education.

Diocese of Louisville

When Mother Mary Catharine took office in 1924, the SCN community staffed twelve parochial schools in Louisville and numerous others throughout the state. In October 1925, fearing an epidemic of infantile paralysis, the Louisville Board of Health closed all schools. Some people said it was a political scheme and that the schools would reopen after elections, which is what happened.

Sacred Heart and St. Cecilia

In 1925, the neighboring schools of Sacred Heart and St. Cecilia formed a united Parent Teacher Association. This organization assisted the sisters with transportation, provided them rides to and from schools in bad weather, and gave them $150 to cover the increase in streetcar fares. In addition to transportation assistance, the PTA also provided milk and food for poor children, and reference books for the libraries of both schools.

At Sacred Heart, in June 1929, nineteen girls and thirteen boys received eighth grade certificates, and beyond the eighth grade, twenty-four girls completed the commercial course. The enrollment for 1932-1933 was 288.

Due to the scarcity of priests, Bishop John A. Floersh appealed to the Canadian-based Congregation of the Resurrection for assistance in the diocese. St. Cecilia Parish was considered best suited for the priests of a religious order.

On March 13, 1926, ground-breaking took place for a new St. Cecilia School. Thirteen classrooms were blessed on December 18, 1927, making St. Cecilia's the largest parochial school in the diocese. The 1932-33 school year listed 762 pupils, sixteen sisters, and one lay teacher.

St. Patrick

The Irish parishioners of St. Patrick's were always proud of their school and church. The children grew up with loyalty to the Catholic Church, in general, and to St. Patrick's in particular. In 1926, the enrollment was 250 and increased to 331 by 1933. In addition to a regular curriculum, both boys and girls had athletics twice a week and vocal training one hour a week. The most talented artists from the art program attended classes at the Art Association of Louisville.

In 1929, Miss Rose Henley, after years of study in New York but affected by the nationwide Depression, returned home to Louisville and accepted the position of organist at St. Patrick's Church. One of her first endeavors was to start an all-male choir to include the boy sopranos with other accomplished voices. This group sang music, such as Verdi's "Requiem" and Mozart's "Ave Verum." Sister Mary Edwina Bailey, principal, and the sisters teaching at St. Patrick's school, took pride in the quality of the girls' choir which sang all weekday masses at St. Patrick's. The younger children's choir also became known for its excellence in music.

The St. Vincent de Paul Society was under great stress caring for the many families suffering from the Depression. Father Peter J. McNeil organized his parish to help wherever and whenever they could, and he set an example by feeding the hungry daily at the rectory. Though a difficult time for everyone, the Irish at St. Patrick's rose to the occasion and worked with their pastor. This service to the needy left an indelible impression on the students.

Catholic Colored High

At the request of Bishop John Floersh, a high school for African American Catholics was opened in 1928. Sister Mary Inez Pigman, principal of St. Augustine High school, became the first teacher in the school and remained its guiding spirit for eleven years.

In 1928, the pastor, Father John Dudine, moved St. Augustine High School from the parish grounds to a new location and renamed it Catholic Colored High School. The historical marker at 429 South 8th Street proclaims:

> Site of Kentucky's only Catholic high school for Blacks in Louisville. Founded in 1928, the school was administered by pastors of St. Augustine Church.

Catholic Colored High School was operated by the Archdiocese of Louisville from that date forward. In 1929, Sister Frances Louise Thompson became a teaching principal there and welcomed Agnes Veeneman to the faculty. At a class reunion, a graduate recalled: "Our school was equal to the best in the country. Nothing but the classics were taught there – Latin, English, French, history as well as algebra, geometry, chemistry, economics, and the arts." Service was also an integral part of the school. The 1932 annals of St. Helena's relate that: "Students from Catholic Colored High School sang carols and spirituals for the residents."

St. Augustine

The greatest asset of the St. Augustine grade school proved to be the establishment of the Parent Teacher Association. Its first activity was to provide a Christmas tree decorated with small gifts for the children. By 1930, the PTA had increased its membership to sixty and continued to be a great support for the teachers. The PTA designed and adopted a uniform for the pupils, and members provided the school with its first mimeograph machine. The faculty increased to five when Mary Jo McGee joined the staff. In 1932, St. Augustine enrollment totaled 240 pupils, with four sisters and two lay teachers.

Holy Name

Until 1926, the sisters teaching at Holy Name School lived first at St. Joseph's Infirmary, and later, at St. Helena Commercial College convent on Fourth Street, a distance of some twenty blocks from their school. The streetcar, their only means of transportation, did not travel to the 2900 block of Fourth Street. Nobody knows how many trips Father Louis Deppen made to the Transportation Office of the City of Louisville to make the case for extending the line further south. When the tracks were finally extended, it was rumored that Father Deppen himself laid the tracks to Central Avenue, a stopping point close to Holy Name School.

In 1926, under the pastor, Rev. John O'Connor, school enrollment increased as he insisted on opening a ninth grade. There was, in addition, a two-year commercial course, the first to be opened in the Catholic schools of Louisville. Sister Catherine Sienna Clark was the first commercial teacher. In 1932, William Cook from the commercial class won a salesmanship contest conducted by Louisville's newspaper, The *Courier-Journal*. The winner enjoyed the prize of a week's vacation in Canada.

Father O'Connor was followed by Rev. Francis Timoney, an expert in both pastoral and practical matters. For years, the sisters had lived in extremely cramped conditions in the small, crowded, and deteriorating Holy Name Convent. Father Timoney decided that time had come to direct the attention of the parish to its condition. One Sunday, in his humorous way, he invited all attending the Mass to walk through the convent on their way home. The children of the four upper grades were likewise invited to tour the convent in preparation for writing an essay entitled: "Necessity of Building a New Convent and the Disreputable Conditions of the Old Convent." It worked. A new convent was soon home to twenty-four sisters. The pastor did not neglect the needs of the school, and 811 students enrolled in a renovated school building in September 1932. Sister Mary Constantia Deitrick, as principal in the 1930s, guided the school to excellence in academics.

St. Philip Neri

One of the oldest parochial schools staffed by SCNs was St. Philip Neri. It opened in 1899 with three sisters and ninety-five pupils. After thirty years, the sisters were still living at hospitable, but distant St. Helena Commercial College on Fourth Street. In 1926, the pastor, Father Edward Russell remodeled a house adjoining the church property and furnished it for the sisters. The new convent changed its daily schedule by eliminating dependence on public transportation. In 1931-32, the enrollment was 240 pupils, with a faculty of five sisters.

St. Agnes

SCNs who taught at St. Agnes School on Newburg Road lived at nearby Mt. St. Agnes Sanitarium. Sister Mary Dympna Francis succeeded Sister Mary Claver Johns as principal in 1926, and she made many needed improvements in the school. In 1927, St. Agnes School was growing rapidly. Margaret Kemper, an alumna of Nazareth Junior College, joined the faculty and boarded at Mt. St. Agnes. In 1931, St. Agnes procured its first school bus in order to transport children living at a distance. In 1934, Ruth Williams, a pupil of St. Agnes, won the honors in the spelling bee sponsored by the *Courier-Journal*. On receiving the plaque, Ruth said, "I am proud to be the winner of this beautiful trophy, not so much for myself, but for Sister Julianna Saunders and St. Agnes School."

In 1934, for the first time, St. Agnes experienced a decline in enrollment. This was attributed to the Depression spreading throughout the country. Despite the hard times, the Passionist priests of St. Agnes parish kept the stories of their mission in China "up front." Consequently, the children's enthusiasm for the Chinese missions grew. Various classes raised as much as twenty-five or thirty dollars for the missions which they excitedly gave to the young Passionist priest who was soon to leave for China.

St. Brigid

After many years of residence at St. Helena's on Fourth Street, in 1928, the SCN staff of St. Brigid School moved to a temporary home closer to school. Within a few months, they moved to their permanent home, the new St. Brigid convent, next to the school on Hepburn Avenue.

In 1925, Frank Neuhauser, an eleven-year-old seventh grade student at St. Brigid School, became the Kentucky champion of the spelling bee sponsored by the *Courier-Journal*. Frank spelled the word, "gladiolus" to become the 1925 national champion and was granted $500 in gold pieces and a gold medal. Upon his return from Washington, D.C., he was awarded a new bicycle which he said he valued more than the money.

The school had been totally staffed by SCNs until 1929 when Rosetta Lutkemeier was employed as a lay teacher due to the increasing enrollments. Athletics was promoted at St. Brigid's. Their track team excelled at meets. In 1932, the boys' basketball team won the championship of the city parochial schools.

Holy Family

Holy Family School had a beginning unlike all others. In 1923, Bishop Floersh requested sisters to teach nearly sixty children he had found running around the barracks near Camp Taylor. The bishop explained that the parents of those children operated a truck garden. "They have nothing else," the bishop added, "No church, no school." The next day, seeking more details, two SCNs went to see him. The bishop pointed out that a two-room building, a former barracks, was available and could serve as a school.

Two SCNs, members of Mother Mary Catharine's Council, initially volunteered to open the camp school. In a short time the permanent teachers, Sisters Mary Casimir Hopkins and Mary Pasithea Yates replaced the volunteers. Transportation to Camp Taylor School was difficult and time-consuming. To be closer to the school, the sisters eventually moved from St. Helena to the newly completed St. Joseph Infirmary.

The children attending the school at Camp Taylor were very needy. Their health was attended to by nurses, doctors, and dentists from the Board of Health. Regardless of their ages, most of these children had never been to school. The children and families also had many spiritual needs. When preparing sixteen children for

First Communion the sisters found that a number had never been baptized. These children were baptized the morning of their First Communion, May 3, 1928.

The Camp Taylor School had been placed in the charge of Father Charles Ruff of St. Elizabeth parish. Seeing the steady growth of the school, he realized the need for a modern fireproof building and subsequently acquired property for a school on Poplar Level Road. Bishop John A. Floersh blessed the newly named Holy Family School on May 22, 1927. In his remarks he said: "The first school I opened on coming to the Louisville diocese... a unique beginning in which the parish will be the outgrowth of the school."

The Holy Family sisters lived at St. Joseph Infirmary until 1932. In September of that year, Sister Lavinia Higgins and four sisters moved into their convent, a five-room house near Holy Family School. The school continued to grow, and in 1932, the enrollment totaled 208.

St. Frances of Rome

The sisters who taught at St. Frances of Rome School lived with the sisters at St. Vincent Orphanage. *The Record* reported that the parishioners spent a proud and happy day when their new school building was dedicated on May 8, 1930. The enrollment was 240, with five SCN teachers. Many people commended the school's orchestra, and its public performances were usually sold out. The sisters often invited the children of both St. Thomas and St. Vincent orphanages to attend matinees of the school's musicals and other events held in the spacious auditorium.

In 1926, Sister Mary de Padua Vaughan was principal. At that time, the Modern Health Crusade of Louisville, in an effort to improve the health of children attending city schools, inaugurated a program of teaching good health habits. The sisters kept individual health records making the activities more like fun. They recorded the children's health habits: brushing teeth, washing hands, getting plenty of sleep. In a ceremony at Fountaine Ferry Park, the noted architect D. X. Murphy, on behalf of the Louisville Tuberculosis Association, presented a silver trophy to St. Frances of Rome School. Accepting the trophy, Father John H. Riley, pastor, said, "The trophy is indicative of the highest good health percentage by the school and also of the community where the school is located."

St. John

Founded in 1857, St. John School was one of the first parochial schools in Louisville. In 1932 the enrollment was 214. The faculty consisted of four SCNs and two Xaverian Brothers. Some of the sisters resided at St. Vincent Orphanage, while others lived at St. Helena's.

First Communion, always a special event at St. John's, was preceded by a three-day retreat. This retreat followed the same order as an adult retreat including instructions, prayer, and an environment of silence. A climate throughout the parish produced a number of vocations. From its founding until the 1930s, nine boys became priests, and twenty-six girls entered the novitiate at Nazareth.

St. Michael

Despite Mother Mary Catharine's intention to open no more schools in cities, an appeal from St. Michael's School in West Louisville caused her to reconsider her decision. Originally for Italian and Syrian children, St. Michael's had been closed in 1920 due to decreasing enrollment. In 1924, the pastor made improvements in the parish and then asked the people what they most desired. The unanimous answer was "to have the school for our children re-opened and the Sisters of Charity of Nazareth to teach in it." In response to this request, Mother Mary Catharine said, "Many places have asked this year for our sisters and I have refused, chiefly because of the scarcity of teachers, but St. Michael's is too poor to be refused by the Sisters of Charity. I must accept." Two sisters were sent to re-open St. Michael's School in September 1925.

During the Depression years, observing the undernourished children of St. Michael's, the sisters and women of the parish worked to provide a school lunchroom. Within a short time, all the children on school days enjoyed hot soup and the favorite spaghetti. The lunchroom was the impetus for organizing a PTA. The parent organization worked on many projects including planning and assisting in the celebration of religious, ethnic, and patriotic festivals.

Around Christmastime 1931, a man with two little girls drove up to the cathedral in Louisville in a farm wagon. He had driven from western Kentucky to look for work and a home for his two children. Through the priests at the cathedral, the younger girl was placed in St. Vincent Orphanage. The older girl, Carrie, went to live with the sisters at St. Helena's and attended St. Michael's School. She had a good mind. Despite having had no formal schooling, Carrie was open and unafraid. With special attention from Sister Laurita Gibson, she progressed rapidly.

St. Monica, Bardstown

St. Monica School in Bardstown had been staffed by SCNs since 1871. In November 1925 a parish mission for African American people only, the first of its kind in Bardstown, was given at St. Monica's by Rev. Cletus Brady, C.P. An early Mass was open to all, but conferences were for parishioners only. Coming from a conference, one grandmother said, "Father Cletus knows many languages but he talks to you in plain language."

In November 1927, diocesan supervisor, Sister Ann Sebastian Sullivan, spent the day at St. Monica's where the older children dramatized "The Pied Piper." Some of the younger children were so charmed with the rat costumes that they said, "Sister, let us have costumes with tails, too!" In 1928, the play, "Christmas in America," was presented celebrating sons and daughters of other countries who became citizens of the United States. The sisters at St. Monica's said they would long remember this play, in part, because Mother Mary Catharine was in the audience.

April 28, 1928, brought an interesting tourist to Bardstown. One morning, as Sister Charles Albert Cruz was preparing the May altar, she heard a woman's voice saying, "When I saw 'St. Monica' over the door, I knew this was a Colored School." Sister Charles Albert welcomed her and learned that the visitor was from Chicago. She showed her through the classrooms where the children were happy to perform with recitations and songs. The visitor thanked and complimented the pupils and teachers. On leaving, the woman gave a donation to Sister Charles Albert who could already picture new hymn books and magazine subscriptions for the library.

In 1929, when the zealous women of the Aid Society from neighboring St. Joseph Parish were given charge of the physical appearance of St. Monica, their care soon became evident. Improvements in the school included fresh paint, a folding door separating rooms, and a better stage. The grounds were improved with playground equipment and landscaping. The children honored the women with an impromptu program of music, drills, songs, and recitations. The teachers were pleased when results of the 1932 *Otis Standard Tests* showed that children of all grades tested were above or in the normal range.

To draw graduates together for mutual benefit, Sister Mary Carmelite Molohon organized the St. Monica Alumni Association. At the end of twelve years, Sister was changed to another school. She had so endeared herself to parishioners that they begged her not to leave.

St. Thomas, Bardstown

In 1914 the Sisters of Charity of Nazareth, after an absence of 25 years, returned to St. Thomas Farm, the place of their foundation as a community. When the sisters returned, there was a warm welcome and great joy. They opened a parochial school, and forty- three students enrolled the first day.

During Mother Mary Catharine's administration, St. Thomas was a free parochial school as it had been since its foundation. A library was started on a small scale and began to grow. Nazareth sent books, and the children raised money to buy more books. Bethlehem Academy furnished bookcases, and soon there were several hundred volumes in circulation. Sister Berenice Greenwell, a noted educator, writing about St. Thomas in the late 1920s noted: "One would need to have taught in a country school to know how eagerly such pupils read when once they have been given the taste for literature." Community supervisor, Sister Ann Sebastian, visited the school in 1929 and was pleased with the progress of the children.

In 1927, the lack of adequate transportation for the pupils who lived a distance from the school was alleviated by the construction of a swinging bridge built over the Beech Fork River. Other schools, however, opened in the area. These schools were evidently closer to home for many St. Thomas students as the enrollment decreased dramatically. The school closed in 1931.

St. Gregory, Samuels

The parish of St. Gregory was located in Samuels near a small railroad station within a few miles of Nazareth. Father Leo Smith, the pastor, asked Mother Mary Catharine for teachers to staff a school. In September l924, Sisters Anine Wehl and Angela Frances Mudd were sent to begin classes in what had been the Samuels Distillery. Forty-four children registered within a few days. Since there was no school furniture, the children used boxes as desks. After hearing about the "desks", Mother Mary Catharine sent used desks from Nazareth for thirty-two pupils. The sisters at nearby Nazareth and Bardstown gathered teaching materials for the new school.

Also of great assistance to Sisters Anine and Angela Frances, were sisters at Nazareth Academy who shared their teaching skills in speech, music, drama, and art. The first graduate of St. Gregory School, Dorothy Samuels, enrolled for high school at Nazareth Academy in September 1925.

St. Gregory School was a typical example of Mother Mary Catharine's devotion to rural education in Kentucky. During her time in office, enrollment remained small, and the sisters did not receive salaries, but Mother never considered closing St. Gregory School.

St. Vincent de Paul, New Hope

The story of the school at New Hope calls for a brief historical note. St. Vincent de Paul School was initiated by lay people, Edward and Anna Bradford Miles. Anna, a student at Nazareth Academy from 1843-1846, was a niece of Jefferson Davis. The district public school in New Hope closed in December 1899. Distressed that education was not available to the children of the area, the Miles couple requested that Mother Cleophas Mills open a school in New Hope. On January 2, 1900 four sisters began classes at St. Vincent de Paul School. The annalist reports that this school was "the gift of Edward and Anna Bradford Miles." The Miles family must be credited with bringing an elementary school to New Hope.

In the 1920s, the sisters started a circulating library. The growth of the library continued as a goal, and new acquisitions were obtained each year. Attendance at St. Vincent's in 1932 reached 134. The school began to offer an additional two years of commercial subjects to prepare students for employment. In the 1930s, the sisters organized a sodality which grew from thirty to ninety members. On Saturdays, the sisters taught catechism to African American children in the area.

The annalist recounts in 1932:

> Nelson County opened a high school in New Hope and employed SCNs as teachers. Much controversy ensued concerning the teachers wearing religious habits in a public high school. The issue, however, was finally resolved and the sisters continued to teach.

Nelson County Public Schools
Sutherland, Culvertown, Balltown

During the administration of Mother Mary Catharine Malone, SCNs staffed three public schools in Nelson County. Enrollment in 1929 numbered sixty-three at Sutherland, thirty-six at Culvertown, and forty-nine at Balltown. Peculiar to staffing these schools was the need for the appointment of teachers by a trustee of the district. John C. Spalding, a Catholic tenant on St. Thomas farm, was a trustee of the Sutherland School. Mr. Spalding signed and presented to the School Board the application for a sister. Only one sister was employed by the Board of each school, and the second sister taught, but did not receive a salary.

Sisters sometimes faced the challenging situation of two teachers sharing one classroom. Equally challenging was the problem of transportation to and from the public schools and St.Thomas Convent where the sisters lived. In 1932, Sisters Mary Jerome Dwyer and Samuel O'Bryan filled out and submitted their applications to teach at Sutherland School. Despite repeated visits to the Office of the Superintendent, the positions were not given to them. Two years later, however, SCNs regained positions at Sutherland School and continued to teach at Balltown and Culvertown schools. Sisters Mary Inez Pigman and Mary Alberta Englert applied and taught in Culvertown from 1932-1935. Enrollment was essential to the appointment of sisters to the faculties of those schools. The sisters rejoiced when, in September 1934, enrollment reached seventy at Sutherland, seventy at Culvertown, and sixty at Balltown.

On December 11, 1934, Father Fitzgibbon told the sisters that a member of the Nelson County Board of Education had informed him that the sisters at Sutherland were to be summoned for a hearing by the Board. Shortly after, Sister Roberta Griesinger received the summons to appear at the County Superintendent's Office in Bardstown. Father Fitzgibbon offered to represent Sisters Roberta and Margaret Joseph Clements, but Mother Mary Catharine advised the sisters to appear in person and speak for themselves.

On the day of the hearing, the two sisters arrived at the court-house. A large crowd from the three schools clustered in the office and filled the hallway. The crowd was a complete surprise to the board. Fathers James H. Willett, William D. Pike and Joseph J. Fitzgibbon were in attendance. The meeting scheduled for 8:30 a.m. was delayed. Father Pike insisted that it begin. The chairman questioned Father Pike's interest in the hearings. He answered, "I am vitally interested in everything concerning school matters, and I am a citizen." After further delays, a woman and her two children alleged that "the sisters taught catechism, bible history, and prayers during the day." As a solution to this, Sister Roberta explained to the superintendent that she would lengthen the school day and teach religion only outside regular school hours. The superintendent was pleased with the outcome of the meeting and to show his sincerity, he brought a teacher's desk for the Sutherland School. Before school started, the sisters signed their contracts and received the free textbooks available for their schools.

St. Joseph, Bowling Green

Sister Mary Dympna Francis, superior, with Sisters Simplicia Dorney and Leona Newman, Mary Fabian Benson and Annette Roth welcomed 130 pupils on September 2, 1924, to St. Joseph School. The music class numbered eighteen.

Beginning in 1925, music pupils at St. Joseph's participated in the June Music Festival. At the conclusion, Professor Strahm of the Normal Institute of Bowling Green was introduced. He gave credit to teachers, pupils, and parents for supporting their children at St. Joseph School. At the close of "The Dance of the Butterflies," Dr. Strahm praised the sisters responsible for the entertainment, commenting: "The sisters sacrifice so much in the cause of education, and their pupils can be picked out anywhere."

Mother Mary Catharine was finishing her visitation of the southern communities, and Bowling Green was included. On May 30, 1929, she visited the school and talked with the children of each class. The pastor gave the children a holiday in her honor.

On June 11, 1929, closing exercises were held and thirteen children received certificates for the completion of the ninth grade. On that occasion Father Felix N. Pitt from the diocesan school office, addressed the youth stressing the need of a religious education as a preparation for any work in life.

St. Joseph, like many schools of its day, traditionally celebrated patriotic festivals such as Constitution Day, Columbus Day, the birthdays of George Washington and Abraham Lincoln. These special days were also marked by talks on historical events and the singing of patriotic songs. In 1931, the girls in grades three through nine exhibited their class work and sewing. The parents praised the sewing as they wanted their daughters to become proficient in this useful art.

At the end of May, the crowning of the Blessed Mother took place in the school hall. The honor of crowning Mary was given to the child who had the highest score in good conduct and in academics during the month of May. One year, Doris Pinkelton, a girl in the third grade, and a non-Catholic, had the honor of crowning Mary.

Holy Name, Henderson

"The importance of learning is to have something to give to others in the future." This was the message delegates were to carry back to their schools from the convention of the International Federation of Catholic Alumnae. With conviction, Dora Manion, graduate and Holy Name's delegate to an IFCA meeting, delivered this message to the student body. The alumnae were active in the school in many ways. Their literary guild introduced the seniors to the Oxford Movement by discussing with them treatises on the Catholic Church by John Henry Cardinal Newman.

By 1925, the graduates of Holy Name High School began pursuing higher education. Graduates excelled at Xavier University in Cincinnati, OH; Notre Dame University in South Bend, IN; Notre Dame College in Cleveland, OH; and Nazareth College in Louisville, KY. Holy Name graduate, Dr. Clarence Manion, Professor of Law at Notre Dame University, was a writer and lecturer of note.

Scholarships and honors reflected the good teaching and diligent work of the students. In 1925, Frederic O'Nann won a scholarship to the Louisville Conservatory of Music. The first prize in the state Latin contest, sponsored by the Kentucky Classical Association, was won in 1929 and 1930 by Holy Name students. In 1932, the Holy Name Girls' Glee Club won first prize in the district and the blue ribbon in the state contest held in Lexington, Kentucky. The PTA and other groups were regularly entertained by excellent dramatic and musical presentations. In 1935, Sisters Catherine Augustine Tierney and Laurita Gibson accompanied the Holy Name High School orchestra which entertained at the U.S. Veterans Hospital near Dawson Springs, Kentucky.

Parents and clergy were proud of their school's accomplishments, and it was a respected educational institution in Western Kentucky. In 1925, the enrollment for grade and high school combined was 255 students.

St. Mary of the Woods, Whitesville

The class of 1924 was the first class to graduate from St. Mary of the Woods High School. Former students recalled how the sisters had privately tutored them in high school courses so that they could get jobs or be admitted into a seminary or nurses' training program.

St. Mary's, a farming community, suffered greatly from the drought of 1930-31 and the Depression . The sacrifices that Catholic families made to maintain their church and school during these years tested and strengthened their faith. Through the vision of their pastor, Rev. Hugh O'Sullivan, the men of the parish baked bricks and constructed a school building.

When Bishop Floersh came to celebrate confirmation in 1928, he complimented the ready responses of the confirmation class. The bishop especially thanked Sister Mary Cecilia Nally's student-organists and the choir for the Gregorian chant so beautifully rendered.

In 1933, rural schools were greatly improved with the installation of electricity. St. Mary's then had a grammar and a four-year high school with an enrollment of 240. In 1925 and again in 1927, the opening of the school was delayed by the fear of infantile paralysis. Despite such setbacks, the enrollment continued to increase, and all rejoiced when ground was broken to add a new wing to the school.

St. Ann, Morganfield

The first meeting of the St. Ann PTA was held in September 1925. The support of the organization resulted in improvements to the building, now a well-equipped school that gave promise that St. Ann's would become a flourishing educational presence in Union County.

In September 1935, school re-opened with an enrollment of 150. With sisters serving as sponsors, student activities included membership in the Agricultural Club, forerunner of Future Farmers of America, and of the 4-H Club. As in many farming communities, St. Ann's students sold seeds to earn funds for their projects.

The sisters attended the area meeting for elementary teachers held at St. Vincent Academy in 1935. Conducted by Xaverian Brothers from Louisville, these meetings dealt with methods of instruction. On their next free day, the sisters visited public schools and found the experience beneficial.

St. Agnes, Uniontown

A quotation from the local paper, *The Telegram*, June 22, 1928, tells the story of how Uniontown got its name:

> On Feb. 12, 1840 an act incorporating the town of Uniontown passed the Kentucky legislature. Prior to that, there existed on the present site two towns: Francisburg and Locust Court with only 200 acres of land between them. The name Uniontown was, therefore, quite an appropriate one.

In the same year St. Agnes Church acquired what was considered the finest church organ anywhere between Louisville and Memphis. Sister Ellen Cecilia Garrity, music teacher, and succeeding teachers of music and choir, trained student accompanists for Sunday, daily Masses, and other events.

A good rapport existed between St. Agnes School and the Uniontown Public School, the latter regularly sharing the use of their auditorium. A demonstration of the Progressive Music Series, used by SCNs as the standard for teaching piano, was presented there also.

The demonstration was presided over by Miss Helen Hurley of St. Louis, Missouri, an instructor for the publisher. She later became Sister John Mary Hurley, SCN.

The inspector for secondary schools from the Department of Education in Frankfort, and the county supervisor visited the high school in May 1926. They commended work demonstrated by students in science classes. The high school, however, could not be accredited until a degreed teacher was obtained for the science department. Enrollment in 1926 for the elementary and high school was 307.

In December 1929, tears of joy and prayers of thanksgiving marked the celebration of Mass in the first convent chapel after fifty-seven years in Uniontown. The sisters could now say daily prayers in their chapel instead of walking to the parish.

In 1934, Father Julian Pieters celebrated first penance by inviting the children to kneel as he sat by the communion railing. Tensions and fears that sometimes make first penance difficult were alleviated. A common practice today, this arrangement was a unique celebration of the sacrament in the 1930s. There were thirty-one in the First Communion class that year.

St. Jerome, Fancy Farm

St. Jerome students consistently entered the annual spelling contest sponsored by the Louisville *Courier- Journal*. A 1927 headline of the *Mayfield Messenger* reads:

> **Fancy Farm is Spelling Metropolis of Kentucky**
> St. Jerome School has sent out ten county champions, one state champion, besides one fourth place in the national champion spelling bee, one second place, and three third place winners in state contests: Margaret Ross, Elizabeth Merritt, Barbara Curtsinger, Edward Ross, Maurice Courtney, William Martin Wedding, Cyril Courtney, Agnes Lucia Courtney.

St. Jerome enrollment for 1927 numbered thirty-four in the high school and 331 in the grade school. In the fall of 1928, Mother Mary Catharine arrived for her canonical visitation. Ever the music teacher, Mother taught songs to all the grades as she visited each classroom. Her great joy was to visit with the sisters in the evening and inquire about their well-being.

On May 13, 1929, St. Jerome High School received notice of accreditation by the Kentucky State Department of Education. The inspector asked in his report that biographies and books of travel, as well as encyclopedias, be obtained to improve the library. To comply with these recommendations, the principal, Sister Mary Martina Stenson, and the faculty accessioned and catalogued 1200 volumes.

The pastor of St. Jerome parish, Father Albert J. Thompson (1920-1935), had experienced the burden of maintaining the rural parish complex of church, school, rectory, and convent. He found himself unable to pay the teachers' salaries and maintain the parish. He knew the solution lay in St. Jerome's becoming a public school. This would require dialogue with the Graves County Board of Education and with Mother Mary Catharine Malone.

Father Thompson's objective was to persuade the Graves County Board of Education to pay the salaries of SCNs with degrees teaching in the grade and high school. There were days of negotiations among Father Thompson, Sister Mary Martina, the Board of Education, Mother Mary Catharine and her Council at Nazareth. Finally, the Graves County Board of Education agreed to pay the salaries of credentialed teachers, and St. Jerome's became a public school in September 1933.

Due to economic conditions in the nation and the devastating drought in the farming community, the parish faced an insurmountable problem - the on-going expenses. To assist in this effort, Mother Mary Catharine and her Council agreed that the lowest salary paid to a sister teaching there would be given to St. Jerome parish. This arrangement kept a qualified faculty at St. Jerome, and the pastor could take care of parish expenses.

St. Charles, Bardwell

Mother Mary Catharine had heard from SCNs in Fancy Farm that the Ursuline sisters had withdrawn from Bardwell two years earlier. In 1924, Bishop John A. Floersh urged Mother to consider the obvious needs and staff the school. Housing for two sisters could be provided at St. Jerome Convent in Fancy Farm. Their transportation to and from school would be provided by men of St. Charles parish. Mother Mary Catharine agreed to send Sisters Maxima Glynn and Vivian Callahan, to staff this rural school that appealed to her desire to assist in rural education.

St. Charles reopened in September 1924, with an enrollment of fifty-eight eager children. The three-storied building had two large, airy classrooms on the first floor, with desks and plenty of blackboard space. On wet or cold days, the school was heated by wood-burning stoves. Country roads, ungraded and unpaved, made difficult the eight-mile trip from Fancy Farm to St. Charles School. Depending upon the weather, the trip from Fancy Farm to St. Charles was provided by a local driver in a truck or a surrey. In the fall, the sisters sheltered themselves with umbrellas from sun or rain as the roads were seasonally hot and dusty, or rainy and muddy. In winter, the sisters braced themselves against the freezing and thawing of deep ruts in the mud, making travel jolting and next to impossible. From start to finish, though, the hardy SCNs lost only one day of school.

"The children were simple, docile, and capable of learning a great deal," Sister Maxima Glynn, teacher of the upper grades, wrote. "In spite of difficulties, God blessed us with exceptionally good health, a proof of the ever-watchful care of God." Eventually, transportation for the sisters became an insurmountable problem; consequently, the pastor, bishop, and Mother Mary Catharine regrettably agreed to close St. Charles School in June 1925. Sisters, parents, and students were saddened to hear this news.

Diocese of Covington

When Mother Mary Catharine was elected in 1924 there was already a long-standing relationship between the Covington Diocese and the Sisters of Charity of Nazareth. The diocese was established in 1853 and comprised of fourteen counties, all within the Commonwealth of Kentucky. During Mother Mary Catharine's entire administration, Most Rev. Francis Howard was Bishop of Covington. He was an educator with a national reputation. The Catholic schools of his diocese were important aspects of his ministry. He appointed a Board of Priest Visitors to go to each school twice a year to assess student progress, methodologies, and the condition of the school buildings. During Mother Mary Catharine's administration, SCNs staffed fifteen schools in the Diocese and a brief, yet unique, educational outreach in the mountains of eastern Kentucky.

St. Mary's Cathedral School, Covington

Sisters of Charity of Nazareth staffed St. Mary's Cathedral School in Covington, beginning in 1856. Most Reverend George Carrell, S.J., the first bishop, praised the sisters:

> The debt which the diocese of Covington owes to these white-capped daughters of Nazareth is beyond calculation. For many years they taught at the cathedral school without any remuneration whatsoever beyond what the parents of the children contributed.

Enrollment of boys and girls in 1932-33 totaled 250 pupils. St. Mary students always received a high number of scholarships. That year, eight boys received scholarships to St. Xavier High School in nearby Cincinnati, Ohio, and seven girls won four-year scholarships to LaSalette Academy in Covington. Records for the early 1930s name twelve boys who entered seminaries; eight of them were ordained. Nineteen girls entered religious communities.

St. Patrick, Covington

For thirty-seven years, the sisters teaching at St. Patrick's had lived at La Salette and walked to school. This arrangement continued until 1928, when Rev. Thomas J. McCaffrey directed the construction of a new convent. Mother Mary Catharine was the first visitor to the new 18-room building.

Sisters from Notre Dame, Benedictine, and Providence Orders, who were preparing for teaching came to visit St. Patrick classrooms. The visitors left singing the praises of St. Patrick's teachers and students.

The St. Patrick orchestra composed of students, ages six to fifteen, caught the attention of the program director at the local radio station, WCKY, Covington. He contacted the music teacher, Sister Bertha Frances Bohannan, and invited her orchestra of youthful performers to broadcast on May 2, 1930. The pastor, sisters, parents and parishioners were proud of the young musicians.

St. Anthony, Bellevue

In 1925, the enrollment at St. Anthony School reached 256, its largest number to that time. For three consecutive years, boys of the eighth grade won four scholarships to St. Xavier High School in nearby Cincinnati.

The well-established commercial course at St. Anthony's was tuition free. The pastor insisted that both boys and girls take the two-year course so that students might have the skills for employment. The music classes at St. Anthony's were exceptionally good when Sister Bernadette Hurst, SCN, a gifted teacher, ran the music department. "The orchestra," to quote music critics, "would do credit to any conservatory."

For many years, the SCN faculty of St. Anthony's had conducted their classes in three different buildings. The parents and parishioners, encouraged by Sister Mary DeSales Driscoll, contributed to a growing fund for a new school building. The pastor, Rev. Thomas L. Coleman, laid the cornerstone for a new school on September 29, 1929, and sessions began in the new classrooms the following year.

St. James, Ludlow

On a hot afternoon in late August, 1924, two travelers carrying heavy bags, Sisters Mary Austin McNichols and Denise Troy, arrived at Latonia, but were destined for St. James convent in Ludlow. As they set out walking, a gentleman stopped his car and offered to take them to their destination. When they arrived at St. James Convent, a distance of several miles from the train station, they were warmly welcomed by Sister Florence Molohon.

One evening in late November, after Benediction at St. James Church, the pastor invited the sisters to front seats in the school hall. In a few words he welcomed them to the "Pound Party," an expression of appreciation for the sisters. After a brief entertainment, the ladies of the parish invited the sisters to the convent kitchen where they found 300 pounds of flour, sugar, coffee, tea, and canned goods.

Enrollment at St. James dropped following the 1929 financial crash. The school librarian, Sister Roberta Griesinger, attempted to lift the morale of the students and their families by encouraging them to read. In 1933, the 250 students and their families escaped from the hardships of the Depression by reading.

On September 29, 1933, at the request of Bishop Francis

Howard, children attending Catholic schools in the Covington diocese participated in the National Recovery Act Parade. This event was calculated to inspire faith in the wisdom and vision of President Franklin D. Roosevelt. The Act promoted reform and recovery by several initiatives such as maximum work hours, minimum wages and a prohibition against child labor. The sisters from St. James accompanied their students on the streetcars to St. Aloysius in Covington where the children joined the parade. The annalist gave an additional reason for the participation of the Catholic children in the Diocese "to show the city officials... that Catholic schools in educating many children saved the state expense."

St. James School, at some distance from downtown Covington, did not receive many visitors. The children, therefore, in October 1934, happily welcomed and performed for the "Palmer Lady," as they called the representative of A.N. Palmer Company. The "Palmer Lady" was a specialist in handwriting. She visited each of the four rooms and observed classes in pen and ink cursive writing, noting, in particular, the proper positioning of hand and arm in holding the pen. The company representative complimented the children at St. James. She congratulated the sisters on the number of pupils who received Palmer certificates at eighth grade graduation and promised the younger children: "I'll be back."

Immaculate Conception, Newport

When Immaculata Academy closed in June 1932, the presence of the Sisters of Charity of Nazareth was not lost to the people of Newport. Sister Mary Edwina Bailey, superior/principal and sisters remained to teach in the newly established parochial grade school, Immaculate Conception, which opened in September 1932. It was a smooth transition from academy to parochial school.

The annals for the 1930s reveal drama and musical performances at the school. The annalist carefully pasted programs in her notebook. For this period of time, there are eight printed programs. Reading the annals reveals many more performances. This was the height of the Depression and the children were involved in selling tickets, acting, singing, playing musical instruments, and selling chances to benefit the parish, especially the school and convent. These fund-raising events also went on in other schools, but we know more details from Immaculate Conception due to the clarity with which these events were recorded by the annalist.

Bishop Howard, wanting to lay a solid foundation for high-achieving youth in the diocese, established two Latin Schools for boys. These schools, one in Covington and one in Lexington, had a classical curriculum. All boys of the diocese who completed the sixth grade could enter the Latin School on the basis of tests conducted each year. Immaculate Conception had boys selected for the school on a yearly basis, often as many as three or four.

The newly installed pastor (1933), Msgr. Gerhard Green, astonished the school children and parents alike by announcing, "Catechism at 2:15 p.m., Vespers and Benediction at 3:00 p.m." This service proved to be lengthy on a Sunday afternoon. The 115 boys and 129 girls, unprepared to sing vespers, recited the rosary instead. However, the sisters, working diligently, soon had the children prepared for participation at Vespers. The following year, the diocesan synod agreed, to the joy of all, that catechism classes on Sunday afternoons were to be discontinued.

Instead of distributing report cards in the classrooms in the usual way, Immaculate Conception school introduced a program to bring parents and grandparents to the school quarterly. Before this audience, the pastor gave each child his/her report card. The children of the first four grades, with report cards in hand, performed songs and recitations for the audience.

Good Shepherd, Frankfort

Since 1917, Good Shepherd School was an elementary and high school in the capital of the Commonwealth of Kentucky. During Mother Mary Catharine's administration in 1929, the State Superintendent of Education pointed out deficiencies in the science department of the high school. In a typical SCN response, Sisters Mary Adeline O'Leary and Antoinette Collins, professors at Nazareth College, Louisville, spent time working with the science teachers assisting both in methodology and in acquisition of equipment.

In 1932, the commercial department and the school library also received additional equipment. One hundred new books were added to the library. The music department received excellent reviews. The boys' choir was declared the best in the city, and the orchestra distinguished itself in competition.

In 1936, the school took part in Frankfort's sesquicentennial celebration. Mary Lawrence Stucker, a graduate of Good Shepherd, was "Miss Columbia." The elementary school children from Good Shepherd who were in the pet and costume parade, won three prizes. An historical drama depicting the history of Frankfort, with 500 citizens as actors, ended the celebration.

In December of 1936, the representative of the *Courier-Journal*, dressed as Santa Claus, visited the city and distributed candy in the public schools, but failed to visit Good Shepherd School. The pastor wrote to the newspaper asking the reason for the discrimination. In response, the promotion manager wrote that Santa's failure to visit was due to a force of circumstances and that he would send candy for every child in the school.

On weekends, the sisters visited the men in the state prison and instructed them. They taught hymns, Christian doctrine, and prepared the prisoners for reception of penance and First Communion. Before the sisters drove cars, they depended upon generous persons of the parish to take them to the prison. A prominent Frankfort lady who had celebrated her ninetieth birthday, told the story of how she considered it an honor to have her coachman take the sisters to the prison in her elegant carriage. In later years, the sisters often walked to the prison.

St. Paul, Lexington

The apostles, St. Peter and St. Paul, were known to have held different opinions. Whereas both schools in Lexington named in their honor followed the diocesan course of studies, like their patrons, they maintained a healthy competition. Within each school, the pupils strove for blue ribbons on Honors Day, and in sports both were strong competitors. The principals of both schools had high expectations for their students.

Sister De Chantal Lavelle, principal of St. Paul's in 1935, was a strict disciplinarian. Her gifts of music and drama, however, were evident in the plays at Christmas, the end of the year performance, and the annual operetta. As often happens, the youngest children delighted parents and grandparents with their unexpected acting. The selection of the dramas and the excellent performance of the cast combined for good entertainment. The enrollment for 1935-36 was 205 students. St. Paul's was proud of its sixth grade boys who, selected by examinations, entered the Lexington Latin School.

St. Peter, Lexington

St. Peter School, under the leadership of Sister Raymunda Rufra from1930-1935, made notable strides in academics and in the arts. Since 1932, it had been known that the pastor, Rev. William T. Punch, wanted the best music in the new St. Peter's Church. For that purpose, he brought Mr. Wulfect from St. Mary's Cathedral in Covington to St. Peter's. Mr. Wulfect, a perfectionist in his art, was a music master trained in Gregorian Chant. He was demanding in requiring segments of practice time that interrupted the school day. A number of parents disapproved the use of so much school time for choir practice. This created discord within the parish.

Sister Raymunda, with the help of the faculty, created a schedule that solved the problem. Singing would be conducted during the noon hour. Boys and girls would each have singing for a half-hour and lunch for the other half-hour. Mr. Wulfect remained in the parish and earned an excellent reputation for himself and for the boys' choir. On Columbus Day in 1936, this choir performed on the radio.

St. Peter's School flourished and, in 1933, had an enrollment of 225 pupils with five sisters teaching grades one to eight. One extra-curricular activity began in 1936 in the primary grades. A missionary club was organized in the second and third grades under the name of St. Peter's Little Helpers. The children elected officers and met every Friday afternoon. They sent clothing and books to the Belle Point and Richmond, Kentucky Missions. They also arranged to have a Mass offered for the poor. At the end of the year they turned over the rest of their treasure ($3.00) to the pastor to use for charity. These children, no doubt, became ardent CSMC members in the upper grades and in high school.

St. Peter Claver, Lexington

In their missionary outreach from St. Catherine Academy, the sisters had a history of association with the African American congregation at St. Peter Claver parish (1888-1927). In his *History of the Diocese of Covington*, Rev. Paul E. Ryan wrote:

> The Sisters of Charity of Nazareth were long associated with the work of the colored apostolate in Lexington, especially through the means of their school, St. Peter Claver. Under

their care, the school always enjoyed good patronage. The majority of the children attending the school were non-Catholic. They received from the sisters solid Christian training and education which helped them toward good citizenship and the solving of racial problems.

Because attendance was poor in the 1920s, and sisters were badly needed in schools with high enrollments, the General Council at Nazareth obtained permission from Bishop Howard to close the school in June 1927. The sisters from St. Catherine's Academy, however, continued to conduct summer catechism classes for the children of St. Peter Claver parish.

St. Mary's, Paris

Since 1888, the Sisters of Charity had taught at St. Mary's School in Paris. In 1924, the school year opened with an enrollment of ninety-two pupils. There were three classroom teachers, a music teacher, and a housekeeper. Twelve pupils graduated from grammar school in June 1925. During a time when a succession of music teachers had to leave due to illness, the music program suffered. In 1926, however, Sister Devota Flynn kept that department alive by supervising the practice sessions of the children. With the arrival of Sister Alberta Lindemann, the music program greatly improved. For a small school, St. Mary's maintained an excellent music department, and recitals drew sizable and appreciative audiences.

In 1925, Bishop Howard gave permission to have a chapel in St. Mary's Convent. Mother Mary Catharine wrote the sisters: "I fully realize what interior peace and consolation it is to have our dear Lord in your midst, and He is all the more welcome as you have been longing for His presence all these years."

Throughout the 1920s and the 1930s, St. Mary's was regularly visited by a member of the Diocesan Board of Visitors. St. Mary's always received commendation, and the children were praised for their relaxed manner which facilitated learning. Reflecting the national Depression, in September 1932, the enrollment dropped to fifty pupils.

St. Mildred's, Somerset

St. Mildred's was the first Catholic school established in the Kentucky-Tennessee mountains. The Catholic population was small and composed almost entirely of laborers employed by the Southern Railroad. In 1926, fifty-two children registered, reflecting a decrease in enrollment. The impact of continuing threats by the Ku Klux Klan in the area was partly responsible for the decrease. The principal, Sister Agnes Bernadine Francis, centered her efforts on improving the elementary school. New textbooks were introduced, and the diocesan schedule was followed.

St. Mildred's experienced a great tragedy on January 29, 1928. Sister Regina Fidelis McMahon noticed that the snow was completely off the roof of the sacristy and smoke was rising from it. Both the church and the school were destroyed by fire. For two weeks after the fire, the sisters lived with parishioners. An old frame building nearby was used for church and school. Eventually the sisters moved into a four-room cottage, and the sixty pupils of St. Mildred moved into a rented building until a new school could be built.

Funds for a new church and school came from an unusual source. The General Manager of the Southern Railroad, and a Mason, Mr. Simpson, came to the rescue of St. Mildred's. He wrote to railroad employees:

> Gentlemen, you may or may not know we had the misfortune of losing the little Roman Catholic school at Somerset, Kentucky, by fire recently where the majority of our railroad men's children are being educated and also worship, and I

am undertaking to assist in rebuilding the same... regardless of denomination I think we should help our railroad families to restore the church and school. Your charity will assist substantially in this most dire distress and coming from a railroad official or employee of an entirely different belief, will make the world a better place to live in....

Railroad employees responded generously.

Mountain Missions

In July 1925, Sisters Mary Gretchen Langenbacher, Mary Germaine Morris, and Margaret Irene England, opened a summer school for six weeks to teach basic subjects and catechism in the mountain region of Belle Point, Kentucky. Having arrived by train from Lexington, the sisters walked for two-and-a- half hours over rough terrain crossing Contrary Creek several times by stepping from rock to rock. They finally arrived at the four-room St. Teresa Mission School.

This was an important educational venture for both the SCN community and the mountain people. At the opening of school on July 25, Rev. H. B. Schulte, director of St. Teresa Mission, offered Mass in a classroom. One of the sisters wrote to Mother Mary Catharine regarding the first day:

> We had quite a congregation – forty people were present. After the Gospel, Father invited everybody to come to school, old and young, he told them it made no difference if they were seven or seventy-seven years old. All were welcome. Several 'older' pupils enrolled.

Major challenges for the sisters were the illiteracy and lack of any prior religious instruction among the people. Five girls lived too far away to walk the distance twice daily, so the sisters set up a dormitory in the loft above the school.

The sisters and pastor were concerned with the health of the people. Arrangements were made with St. Joseph Hospital in Lexington for a doctor and a nurse to give free medical examination. Seventy-five children and adults, Catholics and non-Catholics alike, received medical attention. In response to the sisters' letters describing the situation at Contrary Creek, Mother Mary Catharine sent items such as clothing and candlesticks.

After the first summer, Bishop Francis W. Howard wrote Mother Mary Catharine, "I am sincerely grateful to you for the work which the sisters have done in the little Mountain Mission. A review of their experiences will enable me to decide what should be done in the future." Bishop Howard was not a stranger to the eastern Kentucky mountain missions. He rode horseback from mission to mission and instructed his clergy to move gently in their efforts to evangelize.

The following summer, all eight grades were taught, and for a total of five summers, the SCNs instructed the people at the Mountain Mission of St. Teresa. One young woman completed high school at St. Catherine Academy in Lexington and entered the School of Nursing at St. Joseph Infirmary in Louisville. For several summers the SCNs also taught in the Kentucky missions at Paynesville, Andyville, and Mooleyville.

Conclusion

The Sisters of Charity of Nazareth's educational legacy was most evident in the state where the community was founded. They served Kentucky's city, town, rural communities, and mountain missions. The education of the poor, wherever they lived, was always primary in Mother Mary Catharine Malone's administration. The health and nutritional needs of the poor in those troubled economic times were as much a concern to the sisters as was their students' educational knowledge.

SCN MISSIONS IN OHIO

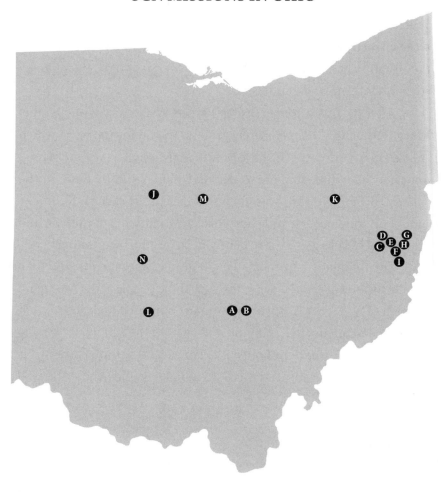

A.	Shawnee	H.	Bridgeport
B.	Corning	I.	Bellaire
C.	St. Clairsville	J.	Shady Side
D.	Maynard	K.	Dennison
E.	Barton	L.	Circleville
F.	Wolfhurst	M.	Mt. Vernon
G.	Martins Ferry	N.	Columbus

Chapter Five

The Ohio Story

T he story of the Ohio Valley is one of hardy immigrants of many nationalities recruited to work chiefly in the mines of Appalachia. The promise of freedom, jobs, and homes in the mining area of the Ohio Valley attracted European families hoping to build a better life for themselves and their children. Families of Irish, German, Belgian, French, Hungarian, Slavic, Polish, Italian, and Bohemian descent brought their strong faith to America.

Mining was a way of life for them, and many a boy dreamt of following his father and brothers down the shafts as soon as he was big enough. While the men worked in the mines, women, with scant materials, but inexhaustible creativity, worked equally hard to make homes out of the row-after-row of company houses. When families gathered to celebrate feasts and passages of life, the women created food, clothes, and customs for the occasion. These strong women, sustained by faith and love, sang the songs, danced the dances, served the dishes, and retold the stories of European roots so authentically that, in later generations, their love and faith lived on.

To teachers, pastors, and confessors, the language barrier was a real problem. Appreciating the immigrants strong faith and close family ties, but recognizing the undeniable disadvantage of their not knowing English, pastors in Ohio rode the trains south to Nazareth, Kentucky, to ask Mother Mary Catharine for sisters "real missionaries," they said. This included a strong request for a music teacher, or "hymn-er," as she was often called. Mother Mary Catharine sent sisters and included in each group a sister housekeeper who would provide a hot meal at the end of the day. Pastors in Ohio had little assurance they could pay the sisters a salary. Scant Sunday collections in many places forced the priests to turn to the sisters for help from school programs and other fund-raising projects. The sisters received little money, but had the enduring gratitude of the people of the Ohio Valley. The memory of her early teaching days in Bellaire helped Mother Mary Catharine respond positively to the priests asking for sisters to work in difficult but gratifying missions, and the children were educated.

St. Stanislaus, Maynard

In 1926, when Mother Mary Catharine visited the sisters at St. Stanislaus School in Maynard , she was pleased to see that there was a chapel in the convent. Sister Anine Wehl accompanied her to the classrooms where 315 children enjoyed her visit, and she taught them songs. While touring the grounds, she was appalled at the condition of the buildings, particularly that of the outhouses. Before leaving Maynard, she spoke with the pastor about improving the buildings.

From the sisters, Mother Mary Catharine heard stories of the experiences of people in the Valley: miners' strikes followed by lockouts; working conditions in mines resulting in devastating accidents; evasion of compensation for injuries by company doctors and lawyers; wide unemployment causing social unrest. She realized that, under existing economic conditions, improvements would come slowly.

In the spring of 1929, a delegation of twelve Polish men and women from St. Stanislaus parish, distressed that their children could not understand English-speaking teachers, met with the pastor. The parents wanted a teacher at St. Stanislaus who could understand the children and whom the children could understand. They threatened to withhold their contributions to the school fund until their request was honored. Aware that he needed the support of every parishioner, the pastor wrote Mother Mary Catharine to explain the situation. Within a week she had asked the multilingual Sister Austina Romanowski to leave her classroom in a Kentucky school and travel to Maynard to teach Polish/English classes to more than a hundred eager children and adults. Sister Austina, full of life, immediately won the hearts of the children and their parents. The children loved this talented, spirited sister who jumped rope with the girls and played ball with the boys. She returned their love and spent almost twenty years teaching a variety of languages in different schools in the Valley.

For five minutes each morning, all classes at St. Stanislaus had mental calisthenics. These "pop quizzes" were on the important facts in various subjects. Special emphasis was put on the fundamentals of Christian doctrine and the common devotions of the Church. Mental exercises also included mathematics, history, and other subjects, as well. The pupils answered readily and intelligently. The facts became a "part of themselves." Years later, they were able to recall the facts that had been indelibly impressed upon their young minds.

Another missionary in the Valley, Sister Rose Dominica Crowley, taught intermittently for 22 years at St. Stanislaus in Maynard, St. Anthony in Bridgeport, and Holy Angels in Barton. On weekends, she also taught religious education at Blaine or Wolfhurst. To reach their weekend classes, Sister Rose Dominica and a companion sometimes left before dawn by coal trains. They had to descend a steep slope and climb up again, an arduous 500 ft. climb out of the valley.

St. Mary's, Martins Ferry

In 1924, Rev. C. A. Mulhearn and the Board of Trustees of St. Mary's School planned to build a new St. Mary's School and auditorium in Martins Ferry. Despite economic conditions of the early 1930s, Bishop J. J. Hartley of the Columbus diocese insisted that a high school be opened and that plans to build a new church move forward.

St. Mary's School of 400 students was staffed by eleven SCNs and Margaret Curran, a qualified instructor of physical education and of dramatic arts. Sister Regina Stickler, superior and music teacher, prepared St. Mary's orchestra for various civic and church events.

The school sports program suffered a major blow in February 1931. The annalist wrote: "Fall of basketball at St. Mary's...janitor ordered to tear down the baskets and break up the bleachers. No more basketball for outsiders. Complaints were made that the hall was being destroyed, and no money was collected for repairs." St. Mary's basketball season, no doubt, ended in February.

In 1932, the debt on St. Mary's delayed the reopening of school. In 1933, however, Mrs. Thomas Dobbins, winner in a "Valley" lottery, endorsed a check for $1,000 and presented it to the pastor, Father Mulhearn, to be applied to the school debt. Such loyalty and sacrifice kept the doors of St. Mary's School open and classes on schedule.

St. Mary's School was closed March 19-23, 1936. Flood waters of the Ohio River submerged tracks of the Baltimore & Ohio Railroad in Martins Ferry and crested at 55.5 feet, the highest recorded there. The sisters received drinking water from a reserve tank that the Belmont Brewing Company shared from door to door, and neighbors brought water from springs to supply them with additional water. Sisters shoveled snow from the back yard and deposited it in bathtubs to melt. Others caught water from the eaves of the school and carried it across the alley in buckets. Working together for the common good was the customary response in Martins Ferry, the oldest settlement in the state of Ohio. Nature led the way in restoring signs of life after the flood. Parents and children cleared their yards of debris, tilled the soil, planted gardens, and sowed the lawns to restore order and beauty.

St. Mary's, Shawnee

St. Mary's School in Shawnee opened in 1891 with 400 pupils. During World War I, the population of the town and school dwindled as military service moved young men and families out of the area. During Mother Mary Catharine's time in office, however, Shawnee was very prosperous because of the coal mines. The children, according to a sister teaching there in 1924, were very intelligent and eager to learn. The music teacher, Sister Agnes Celestine Popham, had a positive effect on the entire population of Shawnee. She taught music to the children who attended St. Mary's School and also had music pupils from the large public school nearby. Those public school children came to St. Mary's for their music lessons. Sister Agnes Celestine had a waiting list, and the parents wanted their children's name on the list before school closed in June so they could start their music lessons when school reopened in September.

In 1924, the Ku Klux Klan had become a visibly threatening menace in the Valley. Dressed in long, flowing white robes, the Klansmen held masked parades down the principal streets of Shawnee. Through their influence, a man pretending to be an ex-priest, held tent services nightly for hundreds of people, mostly from adjoining small towns. One night when he held aloft a small bottle of water, the preacher called out, "Get your Holy Water! Fifty cents a bottle!"

A Catholic teenager, watching the charade and recognizing it for what it was, called back to him, "You can get the real thing at St. Mary's Catholic Church! Free for nothing!"

On the last night of the preacher's stay, the extreme feeling of anti-Catholicism was so threatening that several Catholic men guarded the convent and rectory. About eleven o'clock, the convent phone rang. A parishioner called to reassure the sisters that he was on the alert. Some time later, the doorbell rang. Two Knights of Columbus came to assure themselves that the sisters were unharmed. Gradually, the bitter feeling of that era subsided, and a spirit of trust returned.

St. Bernard, Corning

At St. Bernard School, Corning, a faculty of seven SCNs, with Sister Domitilla Clare as superior, greeted the 1932 school year with an enrollment of 152; forty-one were in the high school. In that same year, when railroad workers in Corning were forced to take cuts in wages, miners went on strike. This had a twofold effect. Company officials removed several trains which left more men without work. Distance and dire living conditions caused dropouts in St. Bernard School.

The miners suffered economically due to the degrading scrip system of the "company store." They were completely dependent upon their employers for food, clothing, and all dry goods. These essentials could be bought only with scrip for exorbitant prices at the company store. Popular at the time was this song describing the miners' plight:

> You load sixteen tons; what do you get?
> Another day older and deeper in debt.
> St. Peter, don't you call me, 'cause I can't go,
> I owe my soul to the company store.

Government agencies set up soup kitchens for school children and adults. The sisters, concerned for the spiritual needs of the many dropouts, provided religious education and sacramental preparation on weekends and during the summer. Ninety pupils, gathered in Kongo, Buckingham, Santoy, and Iron Hill, awaited the SCNs who would come on the coal trains to teach them. Thus, "foreign mission" work close to home was performed before the sisters left for their summer classes at college, or for retreat, or just maybe, a visit home.

St. John, Bellaire

The dedication of St. John's Church in Bellaire by Bishop J. J. Hartley took place on November 8, 1925. It was a splendid event with visiting hierarchy, and native sons, now clergy. The children's choir provided rich, liturgical music. Sixteen SCNs made up the St. John's family welcoming Mother Mary Catharine for the dedication.

In 1924, St. John's had inaugurated a new four year high school curriculum to replace the two-year course previously offered. The school's marching band received special accolades from the Knights of St. George in Wheeling, West Virginia, when they participated in the opening of their convention in 1932. Enclosed with the check for twenty-five dollars was the following note of appreciation to St. John's: "You will be glad to know that the boys by their fine appearance, good music and excellent deportment received general praise and admiration." Intermissions at school plays provided opportunities for St. John's Junior Orchestra to show surprising talent.

As elsewhere in the 1930s, the teachers at St. John's observed adverse effects of radio in the homes. One teacher expressed the problem:

> The radio has changed so many homes into theaters, late hours prevail, and there is absolutely no homework spirit. The music

teachers find the same difficulty. The burden on the teacher is doubled. The general complaint is that the children seem more inattentive and restless than before.

The annual spelling bee, however, created great interest and wholesome competition when Charles Michel of St. John's was state champion. In the national contest in Washington, D.C., Charles placed second. A gentleman present at the spelling bee, when congratulating Charles' mother, said, "Your boy is an excellent speller. Of course, he attends the public school in Bellaire." Shaking her head slightly, Ms. Michel said, "Charles has always been a pupil at St. John's Catholic School in Bellaire." Without another word, the man abruptly turned away. There were twenty-three contestants in the National Spelling Bee that year, and ten of them represented Catholic schools.

Religious instruction at St. Mary's Mission in Shadyside was provided by the sisters from Bellaire. They prepared a new generation of Catholics in the faith. Easter Sunday, April 21,1934, Mass was celebrated for the first time in the new St. Mary's Church, marking the beginning of a new era in the town of Shadyside.

St. Mary's, St. Clairsville
Groups of parishioners at St. Mary's in St. Clairsville gathered for years in homes or in the parish hall dreaming, planning, and praying for the day when they would have their own church. On September 1, 1930, the pastor, Father Stephen Gassman, and his parishioners participated in the dedication of St. Mary's Church in St. Clairsville. Sisters Clemenza Hayden, Patrick Corey, and Mary Timothy Holland attended the ceremony representing the many SCNs who had spent weekends and conducted summer school to teach the young people there.

Immaculate Conception, Dennison

Immaculate Conception School was founded in 1891. Since the parents of sixty percent of the children in the grammar school and twenty-five per cent in the high school were from Italy and Austria, attention to language skills was essential. Economic conditions after World War I seemed favorable for expansion. Consequently, in 1924, the principal, Sister Mary Sidonia Mattingly, announced that Immaculate Conception High School would henceforth follow a four-year curriculum, while maintaining the two-year commercial course. Graduates from the commercial department often obtained excellent positions in railroad offices.

Sister Mary Sidonia was pleased that a high school literary club was organized to acquaint the students with the best authors, to cultivate a taste for good reading, and to enable them to judge and choose good books. The Knights of Columbus initiated a movement to support Immaculate Conception school. They provided two sets of encyclopedias, history and geography maps for both grammar and high school, and an equipped chemistry laboratory.

Perhaps nowhere did the Depression cut more deeply than in mining towns of the Ohio Valley. On March 15, 1931, the pastor, Father Otto Von Lintel, told parishioners that the previous month he and the assistant priest at Immaculate Conception had received no salary, nor had the sisters who ordinarily received eighty-two cents per day. He said that if things continued as they were, the parish would not be able to continue the high school the following year.

In an effort to ease the financial burden of the parish, Father Von Lintel proposed a plan to erect a service station in conjunction with a comfort station for "Ladies and Gents." The site for the building would be across from the church on the four vacant lots owned by the parish. Estimated proceeds of fifty dollars a month from the filling station would help to maintain the high school. The idea caught on. One month later, the filling station was in operation, but it did not bring in sufficient money to cover the ever-growing debts. Ten days later, the pastor told the superior, Sister Mary Clarissa Reith, that the bank had reminded him of the approaching due date on a $4,000 note.

The pressure of financial conditions was visibly weighing on the pastor, and the sisters discussed ways by which they and the children might help. For this to succeed, they drew on an SCN tradition of sister helping sister. Sister James Maria Spillane in Maynard, Ohio, noted for her success in producing programs, gave suggestions. Sister Claracena Burke prepared the first program, and encouraged by her success, the other sisters used ingenuity and creativity with their students. The efforts of the sisters had a twofold effect: the students gained self-confidence on the stage and in working together, and the parish family grew closer as they rallied "to help Father in those hard times." In 1933, the enrollment at Immaculate Conception School was 330; high school students numbered fifty-three.

St. Anthony, Bridgeport

High on the hillside, beautifully located at a distance from the highway, St. Anthony Church in Bridgeport catches the eye of all who pass by. Clergy from every mission in the Valley participated when Most Reverend J. J. Hartley of Columbus, Ohio dedicated the church on January 19, 1928. In that year, twelve boys and twelve girls graduated from St. Anthony School, the largest class in years. The following year, total school enrollment reached 268.

On February 12, 1931, the sisters in Bridgeport joined millions around the world as they listened to the voice of Pope Pius XI. The Vatican Radio Station had been presented to the Holy Father by Marconi, inventor of the wireless.

Armistice Day was celebrated annually at St. Anthony School.

Starting with the morning assembly, the children, singing patriotic songs, marched in ranks to the Bridgeport Monument. The pastor led the parade and gave a stirring address at the ceremony. Public officials were impressed and highly complimentary of the student body. St. Anthony's always received an invitation to return the following year for Armistice Day ceremonies.

In January 1932, a soup kitchen was opened in the school hall for the benefit of the children who were not able to get proper nourishment at home due to unemployment and strikes. The state furnished ingredients for the soup. Everyday the pastor bought a soup bone which the women of the parish used to prepare a nourishing meal.

Aware of the diversity of the immigrant population in the Church of Ohio, the sisters and priests kept foremost in their minds the need to help their parishioners blend into the mainstream of the United States. In the schools, sisters instilled a knowledge and love of the United States, the adopted country of parents and pupils. In addition to teaching the children to sing the National Anthem and to recite the Pledge of Allegiance, the sisters taught them the meaning of words such as "allegiance, indivisible, and perilous." The sisters also encouraged the children to recite the pledge and to sing the National Anthem at home to familiarize their parents with both. The Knights of Columbus strove to strengthen faith in all parishes through unity among the Catholic men.

On March 18, 1936, a catastrophe took place in Bridgeport. Flood waters from the Ohio River rose rapidly throughout the town. Schools were dismissed. Families cleared basements, moved upstairs, or vacated their dwellings. Many parishioners stored their furniture and moved into the parish hall, or joined their neighbors in Red Cross shelters. The water rose to fifty-two feet, causing the worst disaster in the history of Bridgeport. Despite the flood and ensuing debts, faith and fortitude supported the people of St. Anthony's in that time of emergency.

St. Joseph, Wolfhurst

From St. Anthony's in Bridgeport, two SCNs went out daily to teach at St. Joseph's in Wolfhurst. A First Communion service was held at St. Joseph Church on May 31, 1925 for sixty-eight children. School closed on June 12, with seven girls and three boys graduating from the elementary school.

To address language problems, two local priests volunteered to spend their summers in Germany and Poland to master languages. Language barriers occurred even in the liturgy. An incident occurred at St. Joseph Church in Wolfhurst when a Polish priest, wishing to have the censer brought to him, said to the server, "Get some fire." The boy went to the stove, shovel in hand, and turned pitifully toward an older acolyte who came to his aid and showed him how to light the charcoal.

Holy Angels, Barton

Throughout the Ohio Valley, the years of the Depression were difficult. Barton was especially affected by the economic downturn. In 1928, the financial condition of the miners in Barton was tragic. Strikes ended in mine closings, and wages dried up. At Holy Angels, a food kitchen was opened March 26 when soldiers brought supplies of food from the Department of Agriculture. Women of the town prepared daily meals and served those who came. The need for clothing was also addressed. The sisters took care of the distribution of the clothing provided by the US Army.

Nazareth supported the sisters in areas of the Valley where there was no income from salaries or private music lessons. Expressing the sentiments of the Ohio clergy, one pastor said, "May God forever bless and preserve the Nazareth Community for the great work they are doing in these missions." For Mother Mary Catharine, the education of the children and youth was paramount. She made great sacrifices to keep sisters in the Ohio mining district.

Music was important in SCN schools in the Ohio Valley, especially in difficult economic times. The school children at Holy Angels sang a Mass in parts. Boys of the third, fourth, and fifth grades sang soprano; seventh grade girls sang alto and on special feasts, according to the annalist, the children sang the Mass gloriously. Holy Angels School grew to reach an enrollment of 150 in 1932.

St. Joseph, Circleville

St. Joseph School in Circleville opened in 1892, but in its thirty-four years of existence, it never had an enrollment that exceeded 190 pupils. The high school course of studies had gradually been reduced from a four to a two-year curriculum.

In 1924, the students numbered thirty-four, making St. Joseph one of the smallest schools staffed by SCNs. Sisters Laurita Gibson and Raymunda Rufra managed the school while Sister Jamesina Joyce, despite a constant struggle with gas fumes and darkness in the kitchen, cooked the meals. This was a period of bulging classrooms elsewhere and of constant requests from pastors for sisters. Mother Mary Catharine prayed over the decision before withdrawing a sister from any school, but the consistently declining enrollment in Circleville made inevitable the closing of St. Joseph School in May 1926.

St. Vincent de Paul, Mt. Vernon

Aware of a subtle, but long-standing prejudice lingering among some in the civic community of Mt. Vernon, Ohio, Sister Mary Aline Kearns and sisters counteracted the condition by repeatedly inspiring the students at St. Vincent's to strive for excellence in academics, arts, sports, and community events. They knew that the reputation of the school was constantly evaluated against that of the public school system. The sisters, working together, prepared a program of selective presentations to demonstrate for the public the skills and abilities of St. Vincent's students. Mother Mary Catharine was delighted to see portions of the presentations when she visited classes at St. Vincent de Paul School.

In the fall of 1924, the electric company offered prizes for the best essays on "Heating and Lighting the Home." Six of the ten prizes offered were won by students of St. Vincent de Paul, and one essay received national recognition. Dramatic arts drew favorable attention from parents and patrons in 1926, when Dickens' Christmas Carol was presented with authentic costuming and excellent acting.

In 1930, the parish built a modern St. Vincent de Paul Grade and High School. Bishop J. J. Hartley of Columbus, assisted by the pastor, Father William Moran, blessed the new building on September 8. The following day, school opened with an enrollment of 225 students, sixty-two of whom were in the high school. The new building consisted of ten modern classrooms and a combination auditorium-gymnasium to accommodate four hundred persons. Used as a practice area for SVHS basketball teams, the multi-purpose facility served also as the venue for assemblies, recitals, plays, and other events.

The SVHS team won all its basketball games in 1930, including the final tournament game in Columbus, and came home with a trophy. St. Vincent de Paul's James Blubaugh was awarded a trophy for best player in the tournament. In 1934, the SVHS basketball team won every game in its league, and, with high hopes, left for tournament play in Columbus. Sister Mary Vincentia Conlan and SCN faculty joined coaches, teachers, and students at a pep rally to see the team off to victory. At nightfall, the sisters followed the game on the radio. They could hardly believe their ears in the last minutes when SVHS lost. Sister sacristan slowly made her way to the chapel and put out all the candles!

Our Lady of Victory, Columbus

When St. Joseph School in Circleville closed in 1926, Sister Laurita Gibson, superior, in true community spirit, called Sister Mary Alberta Englert, music teacher at Our Lady of Victory, to offer her their music instruments. In her warm style, Sister Laurita ended the call, "Come and see!" Only four years in operation, Our Lady of Victory had a limited number of instruments in its music department, and Sister Mary Alberta was delighted with the additional instruments. She pictured what Circleville's gifts would mean for the music department at Our Lady of Victory.

In 1929, when the pastor dismissed the adult choir and the organist, the responsibility for choir work fell upon school children of the seventh and eighth grades. Sister Mary Celeste Bergdoll worked overtime with a seventh grade girl at the organ and successfully prepared her to accompany the choir. Despite the Depression, the music class reached its full number in 1931.

Unable to pay teachers' meager salaries or the school heating bill, the pastor turned to the sisters for help. In addition to encouraging pupils to participate in spelling, oratorical and essay contests, the sisters and their pupils prepared programs, recitals and plays. Parents and other parishioners joined in fundraising activities. They conducted events such as raffles and garden or card parties.

Aware that the sisters did not attend public theaters, and that few schools had projectors, the Knights of Columbus occasionally arranged with a local theater for the sisters to see a movie. "Anne of Green Gables," and "A Tale of Two Cities" were typical movies shown to the sisters.

Once at the end of a visit by Mother Mary Catharine and

first assistant, Sister Bertrand Crimmins, Mr. Hoffman the janitor, was preparing to take them to the train in the pastor's car. While the vehicle was standing on the inclined driveway, Sister Bertrand opened the car door to put in the bags and accidentally released the brakes. The car rolled downhill. The sisters tried to stop it, but instead, Sister Pauline Elliott fell, causing a flare of excitement. The pastor came to the rescue and brought the car back up the driveway. Another sister innocently opened the car door again, and a second near-accident would have occurred, had not the pastor been there to stop it. Finally they were on their way.

St. Dominic, Columbus

In 1923, through the endeavors of Bishop J. J. Hartley, eighty Catholic Italian children left the public school to attend St. Dominic. The bishop provided money for textbooks for the children. The extra coaching by the sisters brought the children up to par. To the dismay of Bishop Hartley and the sisters, on reaching the middle grades, many pupils returned to the public schools.

By 1925, enrollment at St. Dominic School declined due, in part, to strikes and the movement of people out of the area. Futhermore, racial tensions created great unrest and an ugly spirit in the parish. Many parishioners moved out to the suburbs as the African American population increased in the inner city parish. As a result of dwindling enrollment, commercial courses offered as an elective were closed.

The new pastor, Father Albert J. Fisher, made St. Dominic's a free school and increased enrollment by one hundred children. It was his opinion that no Catholic child should be denied a Catholic education for lack of money. One public school teacher was no longer needed when so many children withdrew from the public school. The public school principal approached Father Fisher and asked indignantly, "When are you going to stop demoralizing [sic] our school?" Father calmly and politely replied, "When I have every Catholic child in my school." Not only did the principal appreciate Father Fisher's determination, she became his ally. She subsequently sent Father Fisher names and addresses of Catholic pupils that he might never have known existed. Each day brought new children to St. Dominic's. Trying to meet the needs of each pupil challenged the sisters as they worked to provide for the newcomers.

Conclusion

Some Sisters who spent years in Ohio found the ministry there among the most strenuous they had experienced. Overriding the physical conditions, however, was the satisfaction found in their solidarity with the people. Language problems and cultural differences presented unexpected challenges. Barriers were broken down with the children's progress in speaking English and the families' participation in parish activities. Singing, dancing, and caring for one another reflected their faith in action.

When asked to describe the SCN influence on the Ohio missions, one Ohio native responded with a single word: "Immense!" and added, "The sisters opened pathways throughout the state with religious education classes which were extensions of the parish and the Catholic school." To paraphrase the words of an Ohio pastor, no group of women ever changed for the better the hopes and ideals of youth as did the Sisters of Charity of Nazareth. There were thirty vocations from Ohio to the SCN Community during the administration of Mother Mary Catharine. This number was a testament to the dedication of the sisters in the Ohio missions.

Mother Mary Catharine Malone
Born: 1861, Yazoo City, Mississippi
In Office: 1924-1936
Died: 1941

St. Vincent Church, Nazareth, KY.

Interior of church after renovation

Most Reverend John A. Floersh, Bishop of Louisville, 1924-1937;
Archbishop of Louisville, 1937-1967.

St. Monica students,
Bardstown, KY.
(l-r) SCNs Teresa
Xavier Williams
Carmelite Molohon
(back) Rev. W. D. Pike

Rev. Richard Davis *(left)*, chaplain
at Nazareth for 38 years
Rev. James P. McGee *(right)*, chaplain
at Nazareth for almost 20 years

Nazareth equestrian party waiting for the horn

Life and Ministry

Nazareth L&N Railway Station

With diplomas and flowers, home-bound graduates leave from Nazareth Station

Countess Spottiswood-
Mackin, Honorary
President of Nazareth
Alumnae

Ignatius Hall at Nazareth College and Academy

Life and Ministry

Camera-ready at St. Vincent Convent, New Hope, KY.
(back, l-r) SCNs: Ann Leo Wilson, Mary Cletus Conlin, Avellino Kelly
(front, l-r) Joseph Inez Head, M. Paschal Fenwick, M. Hugo Crisp, Ann Richard Lyon

Pupils at St. Frances of Rome School, Louisville, KY, and at right, pupils
from St. Vincent Orphanage

Pupils at St. Charles School, Bardwell, KY, dressed casually but took education seriously

Homecoming in August 1937 included forty-two women religious and priests, mostly natives of Fancy Farm, KY.

Life and Ministry

Sister Laurita Gibson, spirited educator and ecumenical enthusiast whose last words were, "Pray that all may all be one."

Sister Mary Edwardine Foose spent years in community service ranging from housekeeping, laundry, and dairy to admissions desk at St. Joseph Infirmary.

Sister Agnes Miriam Payne, R.N., B.S. Nursing Education, remembered for strengthening SCN schools of nursing and also many other training schools

Sister Mary Ignatius Fox, renowned SCN educator in St. Raphael School, Hyde Park, MA (1888-1912).

For more than one hundred years, St. Mary School in Paris, KY, has
maintained the tradition of offering a well-rounded Catholic education.

Graduates of Presentation Academy, Louisville, KY, pose by the side windows
of their dearly-loved school.

Stone Bridge on the National Road in Ohio opened the way for presidents and prospectors, miners, and missionaries.

Mary Hinde-Ball's endowment made possible the opening of Mercy Hospital in Mt. Vernon, Ohio.

"Which hand, Sister?"
Sister Anna Jeanne
Hardesty knew
what was behind
that offer at St.
Peters Orphanage,
Memphis, TN.

An SCN from St. Joseph Hospital, Lexington, making a home visit to check on a small boy's progress after leaving the hospital.

Painting depicting the biblical visitation of Mary and Elizabeth, donated to Sts. Mary & Elizabeth Hospital by a prominent Louisville businessman.

Pupils at St. Joseph Colored School in Morganza, MD.

Statue of Our Lady of La Salette, dear to the hearts of alumnae and students of the academy named in her honor in Covington, KY.

Students dressed for May Procession at Sacred Heart Cathedral School in Richmond, VA.

A welcome break during the summer school at St. Teresa Academy, Rhodelia located in rural Meade County, KY.

Caesar's Bridge over-arching Peter's Puddle was dedicated by the Latin Club of Nazareth Academy on which occasion Father Davis proclaimed: "Caesar ego sum."

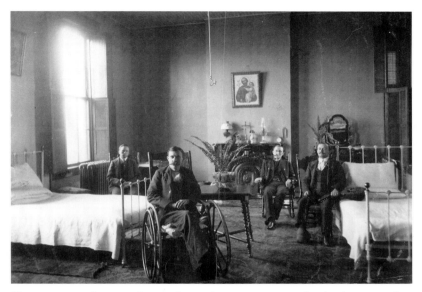

Homey atmosphere in the men's ward at Sts. Mary & Elizabeth Hospital. (Note: man on right laid aside his mandolin for the photo.)

The student body in school uniform of St. Vincent Academy in Union County, KY, posed for the traveling photographer.

St. Vincent Academy Class of 1935 *(Top, l-r)* Eleanor Teresa Hancock (SCN); Helen Schott; Lorena Thomas; Rose Marie Luckett (Martha Rita, SCN); Grace Murphy (Frances Mary, SCN); Elizabeth Greenwell (Agnes Celine, SCN); *Middle*: Dorothy Dickerson (Anna, SCN); Bernadine Tegethoff (Bernadine, SCN); Francis Murphy; Genevieve French; Elizabeth Scott *Bottom:* Nancy Jester; Jane Starnes; Mary Ruebusch (Bernard Ann, SCN); Helen Morris; Elizabeth Hancock (Elizabeth Eugene, SCN); Dorothy Frie

All eyes on the conductor in Roanoke, VA.

Music at Annunciation Academy in Pine Bluff, AR, drew pupils from neighboring states

Sister Mary Inez Pigman, first high school teacher at Catholic Colored High and Sister Frances Louise Thompson, entertained by two former students (names unavailable) recalling stories of their school days.

St. Joseph Infirmary on Eastern Parkway, Louisville, KY.

Life and Ministry

Children relaxing on the lawn at St. Vincent's, Roanoke, VA.

Tired FFA candidates at St. Peter's Orphanage after a hot day in the sun.

Nuns of the Battlefield War Memorial in Washington, DC.
SCN depicted second from right.

Stations of the Cross along the walk leading to the Nazareth Cemetary.

Courses offered in 1933 at Nazareth College Louisville Summer School met the needs of many teachers in public and parocial schools

Opportunity for boys of St. Thomas Orphanage, Louisville, to meet socially with men of the Catholic Orphan's Society often praised by Bishop Floersh for their generosity.

Orchestra at Nazareth College pose before spring concert. Harpist Florence McCarthy, later became Marie Bernadette, SCN.

Chapter Six

Education in Maryland, Massachusetts, Tennessee, and Virginia

Maryland

The mid-1920s saw the flowering of Catholic Education in St. Mary's County in Maryland. With the sponsorship and encouragement of Archbishop Michael J. Curley of Baltimore and of Rev. Lawrence J. Kelly, S.J., Provincial of the Maryland-New York Province of Jesuits, six parochial schools, with SCNs as teachers, were established during that time. The Nazareth mail brought a continual stream of letters to Mother Mary Catharine from Jesuits in Southern Maryland asking for sisters to staff schools in rural areas of Maryland. Aware that sisters could reside at St. Mary's Academy in Leonardtown, she could more readily respond to requests for sisters. When SCNs were assigned to new missions in Maryland, they were in awe at being introduced as daughters of Maryland's own Catherine Spalding. This association eased their entrance into this mission territory, and they felt warmly welcomed.

St. John, Hollywood

SCNs had begun to staff their first parochial school in Maryland in

SCN SCHOOLS IN MARYLAND

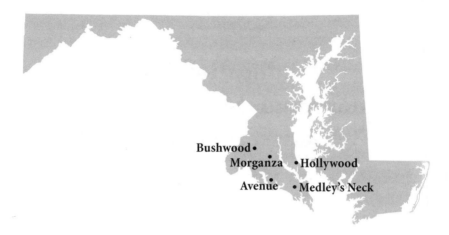

the school year 1923-1924. During the last few months of Mother Rose Meagher's administration, Father Joseph M. Johnson, S. J., announced the opening day of St. John School in Hollywood as September 12. Fifty children were enrolled. Classes were divided into grades one to four which met in the church sacristy, and grades five to eight in the room over the sacristy. Wooden benches served as desks for the students. Sisters Mary Hubert Cronan, principal, and Patricia Rhodes were the first teachers.

The crowded conditions of the classes soon made it evident that more room was needed for the school to operate effectively. The women of the Sodality Union of Washington, D.C., concerned with helping poor country schools, made possible the construction of a new building. In the fall of 1924, shortly after Mother Mary Catharine became Mother General, St. John School, with a capacity of 160, was ready for occupancy. Heating for the school went through an evolution of several systems. Originally each of the four rooms was equipped with a wood-burning heater. Fifty cords of wood for these heaters were stored in the basement. In the afternoon, during the cold weather, the boys carried the logs to each classroom. For twenty years, Father Johnson, S.J., built fires in the heaters early in the morning and had warm rooms waiting for the sisters and the children.

Sister Alice Teresa Wood has loving memories of her father, Albert Wood, and of St. John's. Prominent is the memory of her father transporting the sisters to and from school in his horse-drawn, covered buggy. As a child, Alice Teresa walked with her two siblings through the woods to school. On rainy days, she hurried to be on the roadside when her father passed. She knew he would lift them into the buggy where they would sit next to the sisters.

Our Lady's, Medley's Neck

In September 1924, school opened at Our Lady's in Medley's Neck with an enrollment of seventy-four pupils under the charge of Sisters Patricia Rhodes and Aloysius Gonzaga Roberts. At the close of the year the pastor, Rev. J. J. McCloskey, S. J., wrote a lengthy letter to Mother Mary Catharine thanking her and relating highlights of the first year. "Poverty was the keynote of the hymn of praise our little school was sending up to Heaven," he wrote. He described the home-made desks and benches that filled the rooms and small triangular tables that took the place of the teachers' desks, triangular because they had to fit in a corner and be moved when the door was opened. Father McCloskey added:

> I want to end this letter by thanking you and assuring you that we look upon you as one of our greatest benefactors in sending us such wonderful teachers as Sisters Patricia and Aloysius Gonzaga, and I beg you with all earnestness to permit these same two sisters to come back to Our Lady's School next year.

As usual, providing transportation for sisters and children

to and from school was a challenge. The pastor hired a young man to take the sisters back and forth. Fifteen dollars a month was the stipulated price; then it jumped to twenty, and then to thirty. Before long a donation of $500 allowed Father to buy a Ford bus. Blessed and christened "The St. Gabriel," the bus started on its daily rounds leaving the Academy at 8 a.m., with the sisters as its first passengers. The first load of sisters and twenty children was delivered to the school, and at once, the "St. Gabriel" departed to pick up children from another part of "the Neck."

The spiritual and intellectual improvement of the children was the prime challenge to pastor and sisters at Our Lady's School. The Archdiocesan standard was high and exacting. When examination results were published at the end of the academic year, Our Lady's School had four eighth grade graduates, and throughout the school, most pupils were promoted to a higher grade.

In 1933, when Sister Mary John Horrell was Mother Mary Catharine's companion on her canonical visit, she was deeply moved by the destitute condition of the school. On leaving, she praised the sisters for their ready acceptance of opportunities "to practice poverty in deed and in truth."

St. Joseph, Morganza

In 1924, Mother Mary Catharine responded to a request by Rev. Timothy McCarthy, S.J., pastor of St. Joseph in Morganza, for sisters to staff the parish school in rural Maryland. She sent Sister Julianna Saunders as principal, and teachers, Sisters Restituta Gipperich and Casimir Willett. On September 15, 1924, the school opened its doors with an enrollment of sixty-five. For two months these sisters lived at St. Mary's Academy until their convent was prepared. Not until the Christmas holidays would the sisters have time to paint and scrub the room and restore an old altar for use in their chapel. After it was completed, Mass was celebrated daily.

The parish hall served as a school; classes occupied the gathering space, the stage, and the room above the stage. St. Joseph School lacked sufficient textbooks and other requirements for teaching. With these deficiencies they could not follow the course of studies mapped out for the Archdiocese of Baltimore schools. The students, however, took the Archdiocesan examinations, and most of them received above average marks.

As soon as it was financially possible, Father McCarthy began construction of the up-to-date school he had long planned. At the beginning of the school year, on Friday afternoons, every child was given an envelope to be returned on Monday mornings with ten cents enclosed. This was the beginning of a library fund that, by January, yielded $60.00. With this amount and donations from other sources, books and bookcases were purchased for the school library. During the second year, 1925-26, enrollment increased and a small library became a reality. The children's church singing and stage performances gained for them a reputation throughout St. Mary's County.

St. Joseph Colored School, Morganza

From the beginning of their educational venture at St. Joseph, the Jesuits and the SCNs wanted to provide education for the African American children of the parish. In 1927, St. Joseph Colored School, the name that appeared on the school sign, became a reality. Two lay women, Marie Rustin and Alice Miles, were the first teachers. The annalist noted, "The enrollment was very good for the first year. The school building is a nice one with plenty of light and room. The colored [sic] children took part in the Forty Hours devotion and marched in the procession."

In 1928, Mother Mary Catharine sent Sisters Charles Burch and Elise Bergdoll to teach at St. Joseph Colored School. The annalist described the opening day of school on September 19:

> It was a dark, gloomy, rainy day, the result of which our enrollment was nine. By Monday, when the rain had ceased, and the swamps had dried the enrollment was sixty-seven. The children were eager, once again, to begin their studies. In January 1929, for the first time the students took the archdiocesan examinations and did well. One question was: "Give a line of a poem and tell who wrote it." One young child in the class gave a line of poetry and under it added, "I wrote it."

Sacred Heart, Bushwood, and Holy Angels, Avenue

Southern Maryland welcomed Nazareth sisters for two more schools in 1926, Sacred Heart in Bushwood and Holy Angels in Avenue. Their coming was Mother Mary Catharine's response to a letter from Father Lawrence Kelly, S.J., in which he wrote, "There is not in the whole county a field so promising in the number of Catholic children as Holy Angels in Avenue and none so much in need of a Catholic school because of Protestant activity in this area." His request was exactly what Mother had in mind in sending sisters to work with needy children.

Living accommodations at St. Mary's Academy would not be needed for these sisters. The Jesuits had been bequeathed Bushwood Manor, a beautiful colonial mansion for use in the furtherance of Catholic education in Maryland. Bushwood Manor, however, once the showplace of the county, was in deplorable condition. For weeks the work of clearing the mansion provided fun and a means of bonding among SCNs in Maryland. Beginning in the attic, they threw out truckloads of rubbish. As closets, chests and trunks were opened, there were many surprises, even Civil War uniforms. Classrooms for Sacred Heart School and living quarters for both faculties were suitably established and readied for the opening of Sacred Heart School in

Bushwood and Holy Angels School in Avenue in September 1926.

The schools opened with an enrollment of eighty pupils at Sacred Heart and 157 pupils at Holy Angels. The first faculty at Sacred Heart consisted of Sisters Mary Redempta Adkins and Mary Louise Hils. Two sisters forming the faculty at Holy Angels were Sisters Ambrose Clark and Domitilla Clare.

Years later, on January 3, 1934, Sister Maxima Glynn, missioned in Bushwood, answered the doorbell at Sacred Heart Convent. She welcomed the two eighth grade boys who asked to see the Christmas crib in the sisters' chapel. When Sister Maxima turned on the lights at the crib, the dry cedar tree immediately burst into flames. The fire spread quickly and soon enveloped the entire manor. Despite the efforts of Mr. Johnson, a parishioner who crawled through smoke to the chapel door, it was too late to save the Blessed Sacrament. The sisters felt their hearts breaking as they witnessed their home burning to the ground. Realizing they could not help, they hurried to Sacred Heart Church to seek God's protection.

When word of the fire reached St. Mary's Academy, Sister Mary Aline Kearns immediately sent the bus to Bushwood to bring the saddened sisters back to St. Mary's where they were received with open arms. Until other arrangements could be made, the Bushwood and Avenue sisters commuted daily from St. Mary's. Later, vacant rooms at Holy Angels School were converted into a temporary convent for both faculties.

Finally, the sisters of both schools happily moved into a new three-story convent in Avenue. The pastor, Rev. J. Rudtke, S.J., told the sisters that after his retreat he had stopped in to see Archbishop Michael J. Curley, and shared with him his eagerness to settle the debt on the convent. The bishop asked how much he owed and as Fr. Rudtke left, he handed him a check for $3,000. This was the amount needed to liquidate the debt and was Archbishop Curley's second gift in the same amount. Father Rudtke's hope to pay for the convent at Holy Angels, Avenue, was at last realized.

In 1934, the parish priest at Holy Angels obtained a bus to provide transportation to St. Mary's Academy for the girls who had graduated from Holy Angels. The bus also transported parishioners to parish functions such as catechism classes, Forty Hours, novenas, picnics, festivals and tournaments.

SCN SCHOOLS IN MASSACHUSETTS

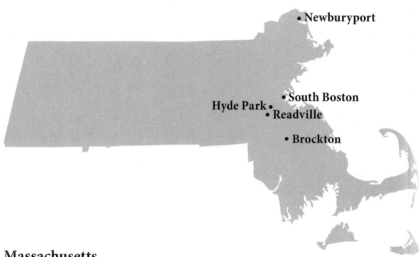

Massachusetts

Since 1883, when the first SCNs arrived as teachers in Newburyport, Massachusetts, the Sisters of Charity of Nazareth developed mutual bonds of respect and affection with students and their parents. The SCNs, having come from such a distance, initially seemed like foreigners. Their religious habit, complete with an adaptation of a Kentucky sunbonnet, differed from the familiar religious habits to which the people were accustomed. The slower Kentucky accent contrasted strongly with the clipped New England speech. Although distance, dress, and accent at first created a psychological "barrier," it gradually dissolved. Happy, faith-filled, intellectually curious children became the best advertisement of the SCNs as an educational community. The progress made in SCN schools was recognized and valued by parents and clergy alike.

Catholics parents in Massachusetts, mostly Irish, valued a religious vocation and were not hesitant to entrust their daughters to become Sisters of Charity of Nazareth. During the administration of Mother Mary Catharine, sixty-four young women entered the novitiate at Nazareth.

Immaculate Conception, Newburyport
From the opening of Immaculate Conception School in 1882, pupils each year registered in ever-increasing numbers. Teaching was rewarding as parents cooperated and encouraged the children to achieve. The sisters took great interest in their pupils and followed their progress and achievements with prayer and genuine interest.

Very early on Christmas morning in 1924, the sisters at Immaculate Conception Convent were awakened by a rich tenor voice singing "Adeste Fidelis." It took but a short time for the sisters to realize they were listening to John McCormack, the popular Irish tenor. Each Christmas, the Knights of Columbus gave the sisters a gift. That year's gift, a radio, was carefully hidden by Sister Mary Gerard McDermott, superior, until the propitious moment to let it announce Christ's birthday.

On March 7, 1927, a devastating fire threatened Immaculate Conception School. The fire, stemming from an unknown cause, began in the ceiling of the auditorium and worked its way into the classrooms above. Capable firemen soon had the flames confined preventing the fire from making much headway. In tracing the fire's origin, the firemen were obliged to rip up sections of the classroom flooring. That, along with water damage, caused the greatest loss.

School remained closed, however, for only one week.

Newburyport's colorful leaves lent a picturesque welcome to Mother Mary Catharine and Sister Mary Evarista Healey, when they arrived for a four-day visit in October of 1927. Mother Mary Catharine was charmed by the beauty of New England and never lost the chance to delight the sisters by telling them so. She declared Newburyport to be "Nazareth's pioneer mission in the East" and in a later communication called it "Nazareth's Cradle of the East." A compliment came to Mother Mary Catharine when His Eminence, William Cardinal O'Connell, during a visit to Immaculate Conception, told the pastor how fortunate the parish was to have SCNs teaching in its school.

On August 31, 1932, the total eclipse of the sun darkened New England at the exact projected time, 3:22 p.m. A black shadow cut in on the sun's surface, gradually lessening sunlight although it was moving at 2000 miles per hour, or so they had been told by amateur astronomers. All of nature was affected by the phenomenon. Even the birds flew hither and thither, and the water in the ocean turned a pale yellow.

St. Raphael, Hyde Park

Sister Anna Louise Mattingly, principal and an experienced educator, continued the intensive in-service teacher training program begun by her predecessor. Ever vigilant for ways and means of improving the quality of instruction within the school and the expansion of competence of her teachers, she took advantage of each available opportunity. On Saturdays and holidays, she invited specialists in various fields to instruct the sisters and thus to lift ever higher the standards of excellence at St Raphael School. Accordingly, the Supervisor of Music in the Boston School System was engaged to give instructions in sight reading and vocal exercises. Sister Anna Louise employed the Supervisor of Drawing from the Boston Public Schools to give lessons in art and to oversee lesson plans for each grade.

She arranged an elocution teacher for speech, a feature of which was short floor talks given by the sisters on Sunday evenings in the convent community room. The theme of the talks varied from personal experiences to the rise and development of modern industries, to early days of the missions in mining districts, to the biographies of great presidents. The music teachers also took part in the floor talks. One traced the history of bells from their origins to the Westminster chimes in St. Vincent Church at Nazareth, Kentucky. Another music teacher researched the history and development of Gregorian chant and its impact on the liturgy.

Never in the history of the nation had a presidential campaign aroused such intense and widespread interest as that of 1928. Naturally, the sisters of Hyde Park followed with prayers every step of Alfred E. Smith's campaign. Sister Anna Louise and the sisters were grateful when members of the Democratic Committee offered to take any sister not yet registered to the proper precinct and to provide all with rides to the polls on Election Day. However, the sisters were disappointed when they learned that His Eminence, William Cardinal O'Connell, strongly disapproved of their voting. Sister Anna Louise wrote to Mother Mary Catharine who responded that the sisters should follow the wishes of the Cardinal. A few days later, in another letter, she wrote that after prayerful discernment she had changed her mind. Mother Mary Catharine believed the rights given by the 19th Amendment granting women the right to vote should prevail. She encouraged the sisters to vote.

To crown her years of teaching elementary and junior high pupils, Sister Anna Louise fulfilled a dream of compiling poems of literary value for junior high pupils. On March 25, 1930, each sister at St. Raphael Convent in Hyde Park found at her place at the dining table a pre-publication copy of Sister Anna Louise's work, *Poetry for Junior Students* by a Sister of Charity of Nazareth, 1931.

No story of St. Raphael, Hyde Park would be complete without mention of St. Catherine, Corriganville, near Hyde Park. To alleviate crowding at St. Raphael, children in grades 1-6 who lived in the area of Corriganville attended St. Catherine, a four room school. Combined grades occupied three of the rooms, and the fourth was used for plays, parties, and other activities. There was an annual May procession combined with St. Raphael. The children practiced marching for a week prior to the event. Instructions from the sister in charge evidenced competition with St. Raphael as she told the children: "Our lines will be straighter than St. Raphael's. St. Catherine's will be the best of all the groups."

St. Anne, Readville

The new parish, St. Anne's in Readville, which opened in 1922, relieved the overflowing enrollment at St. Raphael's School in Hyde Park. The pupils, who transferred to St. Anne's brought with them the high standard of learning characteristic of St. Raphael's. The original faculty, still revered, included Sister Rose Vincent Harrington, principal, who stayed for twelve years; Sister Reparata Hagarty, who was noted as a legendary primary teacher, and Sister Francis Borgia Quigley, an excellent teacher. In 1931, the original convent building was enlarged with the addition of seven rooms and the construction of a chapel.

On October 8, 1925, the sisters at St. Anne's warmly welcomed Mother Mary Catharine for a visitation. The pastor, Father David Regan, accompanied her to each classroom, praising the work of the sisters. He pointed out that, though the youngest and most humble in surroundings, St. Anne ranked favorably with the largest parishes in the diocese. St. Anne's boys took three of the four scholarships awarded to Boston College High School that year. Father Regan added that the sisters were edifying religious and that, without them, Readville would not have kept the faith during the years when families lived far from church. He concluded, "No one but God would ever know what a support the sisters had been to pastors and to the parish." Mother Mary Catharine was impressed with his sincerity.

The next day, accompanied by Sister Mary Anicetus Kennedy, Mother Mary Catharine visited Cardinal O'Connell, and he, too, congratulated her on the good work the sisters were doing. He stated that the priests always spoke of the sisters as "self-sacrificing, hard-working, and good religious." He praised Sister Mary Anicetus "particularly for your work in the struggling parish of St Anne."

Some years later *The Pilot* carried an article by Father Peter Conley about the sisters who had taught at St. Anne's, Readville. In the article he also paid tribute to all sisters in the U.S.A:

> It must always be remembered that religious women were of greater influence in building the Church in the United States than bishops and priests. They were not only more numerous, the sisters were also more visible, more available, and more formative in their educational contact with generations of students. It is a debt that can never be fully paid.

St. Anne Parish rejoiced on September 24, 1926, when one of their alumni, Joseph Meaney, was ordained for the Maryknoll Mission Society. Joseph Meaney, M.M., was the first recipient of the Mother Catherine Spalding Burse for the education of a missionary priest. He thanked the SCNs who represented Nazareth at his ordination and promised prayers for the congregation.

Nazareth High School and Grammar School, South Boston
At the beginning of the administration of Mother Mary Catharine,

Sister Emiliana Murray and a faculty of twenty-two, including six lay teachers, maintained high standards of education at Nazareth High School and Grammar School in South Boston. Sister Mary Regina O'Farrell, principal from 1927-1933, and Sister Rose Angeline Ogg, principal from 1933-1939, continued the excellent curriculum at Nazareth School. The high school offered both classical and commercial courses of study. Some parents, forseeing the opportunity to prepare their children for a career in public service, politics or law, paid an extra fee for classes in oratory and public speaking.

Father Mortimer Twomey did everything in his power to encourage education among the children of his parish. There were no fees, and books were free. Children paid only for paper and pencils and five cents per week if they took elocution class. Father Twomey's classes in Shakespeare were so successful that students saved their candy money and did odd jobs to pay for tickets to Shakespearean plays in Boston.

In February, 1933, when Rev. P.J. Waters was pastor, a fire destroyed St. Eulalia's Church for a second time (the first fire was February, 1916). Nothing remained of the original structure. On a nearby site, the church was rebuilt and renamed St. Bridget.

On June 20, 1934, Philip A. Fuhs, S.J., the first graduate of Nazareth Grammar School to enter the Jesuit Society, was ordained. His SCN sisters, Margaret Eulalia and Philip Maria, attended the ceremony.

In May 1936, honors came to the high school and initiated correspondence between Nazareth, Kentucky and Nazareth School, South Boston. Sister Rose Angeline wrote to Mother Mary Catharine: "This is one of the grandest contests that has been held in Massachusetts for high schools. Miss Bernice McGrail is our school champion, She was the only Catholic High School representative..." Mother Mary Catharine evidently wrote to congratulate the pastor, Rev.

P.J. Waters who responded, "The victories in Spelling and in Oratory made our High School the subject of very favorable criticism all through the state...."

Among the teachers who endeared themselves to the girls at Nazareth High School was Sister Louise Rabold. Her teaching style with dramatic, exaggerated gestures was long remembered by her students.. In order to help the girls gain poise and grace, she led them in what she called "feather movements" around the room. With her fingers uplifted and her voice raised to a falsetto, Sister Louise led, "With fingers, always leading..." Years later when Southie girls got together, they reenacted this scene from her classes. They formed processions, lifted their voices to a dramatic lilt, struck an arabesque pose to attain the feather movements as they imitated Sister Louise. A self-chosen leader called out, "Now, follow me, girls. Always lead with the fingers." Whatever that lesson was supposed to teach, it lived within the women they became and gave them grace and poise in posture and step.

During Mother Mary Catharine's administration, Nazareth School's student body was quite large. The enrollment for 1931-32 was 429 boys and 611 girls.

St. Patrick, Brockton

In June 1925, one thousand guests attended the first graduation held in the new auditorium at St. Patrick School in Brockton. *The Brockton Times* gave credit to the Sisters of Charity for what the reporter described as "the most beautiful graduation exercises ever staged in this city."

During her years in charge of St. Patrick School, Sister Dorothea Creeden had expanded the curriculum to include elocution. Pupils found their voices as their speech teacher directed them in recitations and performances for a nominal fee of five cents a week. Together with the music teacher, the elocution teacher directed operettas and plays for the enrichment of the children and the enjoyment of parents and friends. The pastor, Father J. P. Gill, endorsed physical education for all classes.

Among the pupils of St. Patrick's who excelled in musical performances was Florence Burke, later Mary Walter Burke, SCN, an outstanding member of the faculty at Presentation Academy in Louisville. She received a Bachelor of Music degree from the Louisville Conservatory of Music and a Master's degree from the College of Music in Cincinnati. While at Presentation Academy, Sister Mary Walter repeatedly accommodated Nazareth College, SCN academies, and high schools by composing a school song. Someone described her as a cheerleader whose rousing compositions called one to join the beat, strike up the band, give a cheer, and sing "We're the best school in the land!"

In addition to their daily work at St. Patrick School, the sisters took charge of weekend religious education classes in many surrounding parishes: St. Edward and St. Margaret in Brockton; St Michael in Avon; St. Joseph in Holbrook; St. Thomas Aquinas in Bridgewater; Holy Ghost in Whitman; and Holy Rosary in Stoughton.

On August 10, 1927, the local community celebrated the fortieth anniversary of the arrival of SCNs from Nazareth, Kentucky. Sister Anacleta McQuade, the last of the original band of eight still at St. Patrick's, prompted Sister Ann Sebastian to say: "Sister Anacleta is a part of Brockton!" That year Nazareth sent eight sisters to teach in Brockton and, coincidentally the same year, seven young women from Brockton entered the novitiate at Nazareth. The attendance at St. Patrick's from its beginning in 1896 remained steady through the years that Mother Mary Catharine was in office. In 1896, St. Patrick's had an enrollment of 536 students and in June 1927 there were 558 students, sixty- three of whom were in the high school.

SCN SCHOOLS IN TENNESSEE

•Memphis

Tennessee

May 18, 1929, will ever be remembered by the Catholics of Memphis. A monument, erected to the memory of the sisters who gave their lives nursing the yellow fever epidemics of 1873, 1878, 1879, was unveiled at the Catholic Club. The ceremony was planned for Calvary Cemetery but inclement weather prevented using the site.

During Mother Mary Catharine's administration, four schools, all in the city of Memphis, were staffed by SCNs. Ten young women from Memphis entered the novitiate at Nazareth.

St. Brigid, Memphis

On September 9, 1932, St. Brigid School, in Memphis, under the principalship of Sister Thomasine Clary, opened the new school year. The first day the enrollment was 140 pupils. Installation of slate boards and freshly painted classrooms invited teachers and pupils back to school.

St. Brigid Grammar School graduated thirteen students on June 13, 1933, and fourteen the next year. Despite hard times, the penny socials in November and May netted $816. This reflected the loyalty and love of the parents and pupils for St. Brigid School. To prepare themselves for service on the safety patrol at St. Bridgid, the boys even attended safety classes on Saturdays.

Sisters and altar boys from St. Brigid Church took part in the service of dedication of the Poor Clare Monastery in Frasier, Tennessee. The sisters prepared the children for two May processions, one at St. Brigid Church in Memphis and the other at Our Lady of Sorrows Church in Frasier.

SCNs inherited from St. Peter's Orphanage a reputation for hospitality, and, during Christmas vacation, the sisters at St. Brigid helped to maintain it. On Holy Innocents Day they entertained the religious of Memphis, and newcomers to Memphis welcomed the hospitable atmosphere there. One afternoon two cars took the St. Brigid SCNs to the new convent of the Sisters of Charity of the Blessed Virgin Mary (BVM) from Dubuque, Iowa. The BVMs had opened St. Augustine School for African American pupils in September. The SCNs and BVMs enjoyed a lively exchange. SCNs complimented the BVMs on the progress evident in their pupils in three months. Two days later the priest from St. Michael's arranged a bingo for all sisters. Many attended less for bingo than for conviviality of the season. On another day, the Christian Brothers invited all religious to a movie at their college. The holidays provided multiple opportunities for the religious of the area to know, appreciate, and support one another in their ministries. New Year's Eve at St. Brigid's, as in all SCN convents, was traditionally observed as a day of silence and recollection.

St. Patrick, Memphis

In April 1925, Bishop Alphonse J. Smith, Bishop of Nashville, blessed the site for a new school building. To the joy of all, the school was ready by September 1925, and staffed by five sisters and a music teacher.

During Mother Mary Catharine's administration, a letter dated August 1, 1929 came from the pastor, Father Hayes. He explained that there was a regular exodus of families from St. Patrick's which he said: "is characteristic of every downtown section throughout the country." His letter also informed her that four sisters would be sufficient for the 150 students expected in September. When Sister Mary Constantia Deitrick was principal, the school had a reputation for excellence. Since December 1931, sisters who taught at St. Patrick's lived at St. Peter's Orphanage. For that year the enrollment was 107. By 1934, the faculty was reduced to three sisters who taught multiple grades.

Sacred Heart, Memphis

In 1924, Sacred Heart School opened with an enrollment of 450. Seven seniors and twenty-nine eighth grade pupils graduated in June 1925. Sisters Agatha Young, Mary Thomasine Dymond and Mary Edwina Bailey served successively as principals from 1923-1938. During that time uniform textbooks were adopted for the schools in the Diocese of Nashville. The SCNs rejoiced when five high school graduates entered the Nazareth Novitiate.

Father Louis J. Kemphues, the pastor, trained the children for marching in the annual Armistice Day Parade. As a result of his efforts, Sacred Heart School received an award for the best parochial school drill team.

During a visit with Most Reverend A. J. Smith, Bishop of Nashville, in February 1930, Rev. Louis J. Kemphues obtained the long-desired permission to build a school. Sacred Heart School, a large three-story building housing sixteen large classrooms and a cafeteria, was completed in 1933. A newspaper reporter described the new elementary and high school as a "magnificent structure acclaimed second to none in the country." The article continued, "the school building is admirably adapted to the needs of the time... Following the plan laid out by the pastor, Father Kemphues, the design of the building is a delight to the eye." Naturally, the finely-equipped school attracted students, and the enrollment increased to 425 in the elementary school and 165 in the high school. The original combination church-school building was razed.

Little Flower, Memphis

Little Flower School was an offspring of St. Brigid School in 1930, with membership drawn mainly from St. Brigid parish. The Sisters of Charity of Nazareth continued to live at St. Brigid until a convent was opened at Little Flower in 1937. Sister Thomasine Clary was superior at St. Brigid when the new parish was established.

The Church of St. Therese of the Infant Jesus, was affectionately called Little Flower for its patroness. The name has a history of inconsistent spelling, at times Teresa, other times, Therese or Theresa. The church was the first in Tennessee to be named for the Little Flower who was canonized only five years before the parish was established. Its founding in 1930, at the peak of the nation's Great Depression, may have seemed foolhardy. Despite the national economy, Most Reverend Alphonse J. Smith, Bishop of Nashville, authorized the building of St. Therese Church and appointed Rev. James Whitfield, the pastor of St. Brigid's Church, to oversee the construction of the elementary school.

"For God and Country!" Rev. J. P. Whitfield may have exclaimed as he planted the country's flag near the spot where he had turned the first spade of earth for the new church in northern Memphis. It was March 25, 1930, and Father Whitfield had finally procured from Mother Mary Catharine the promise of four Sisters to staff the new school. In the record time of six months, the school building was ready for the opening on September 15, 1930.

SCN SCHOOLS IN VIRGINIA

Richmond •

• Roanoke

Newport News

Virginia

In 1893, at the request of Most Rev. Augustine Van De Vyver, Bishop of the Diocese of Richmond, Mother Helena Tormey sent sisters to Virginia. Six sisters arrived in Roanoke to teach at St. Andrew School, the initial foundation by SCNs in the state of Virginia. In less than a month, St. Vincent Home for Boys also opened in Roanoke. These early sisters commented often on the beauty of Roanoke, set in a valley surrounded by the Appalachian Mountains.

SCNs began teaching at the Cathedral Parish in Richmond, in 1901. It was the capital of the Confederacy during the Civil War, and numerous monuments throughout the city commemorate the southern leaders of that war. St. Vincent de Paul School, staffed by SCNs, opened in 1903 in Newport News. Shipbuilding was the leading industry and employed thousands. In the early 1900s, the Newport News shipyard was the second largest in the world. When the sisters first arrived, they were mistaken by some as dry dock employees. In their traditional black habits, the sisters were also thought to be mourners. Seeing the sisters for the first time, employees asked if the president of the shipyard had died. During the administration of Mother Mary Catharine, nineteen young women from Virginia entered the novitiate at Nazareth.

St. Andrew, Roanoke

The leadership of St. Andrew School and of St. Vincent Orphanage in Roanoke under one superior ended in 1929. Sister Soteris Muennich was named superior of St. Andrew's, and Sister Mary Pierre Byrne became superior of the Orphanage.

In 1931, the Virginia Chapter of the IFCA stated that, at the next convention, all secondary schools should be one hundred percent accredited. For full certification in Virginia, all teachers were required to take prescribed courses taught at Virginia Technical Institute in Blacksburg. After teaching all week, the faculty at St. Andrew's traveled fifty miles for the certification classes. In 1932, St Andrew's School achieved accreditation from the state of Virginia.

Sister Mary Charlesetta Bowen, teacher of health and physical education to the freshman class, was pleased with the gift of a new RCA record player. Sister found it valuable for marching, drills, and for physical education classes. Her classes reached notable efficiency in dashes, running, and jumping. When Sister Mary Charlesetta appeared in the classroom to teach a hygiene class, one precocious boy asked, "Sister, where's your whistle?"

Vincent S. Waters, a graduate of St. Andrew's School, left on September 15, 1928, to begin his studies for the priesthood at the North American College in Rome for the Richmond diocese. The following year, Pope Pius XI graciously bestowed his apostolic blessing on the sisters and students at St. Andrew's and for those at St. Vincent's Orphanage. The blessing was, no doubt, obtained by Vincent Waters for his alma mater and the boys at the orphanage. (In 1945, Rev. Vincent Waters was consecrated Bishop of Raleigh, North Carolina.)

During the month of July 1929, an epidemic of infantile paralysis created a scare in Roanoke and the surrounding area, causing great concern among the public health officials. "Stay in your own yard," became the slogan. Summer resorts and places of amusement were closed to children, and those under sixteen years of age were not permitted to leave or enter the city. Schools delayed opening until late October when the quarantine was lifted.

After a program presented by the children of St. Andrew's in December 1929, Mother Mary Catharine, in her characteristic way, told, in a few words, how much she had enjoyed her visit to Roanoke: "How much more beautiful than all nature's scenery surrounding Roanoke, are the faces of St. Andrew's pupils which mirror the image of their Creator."

On September 23, 1934, the centenary of Catholicity in Roanoke was celebrated at St. Andrew's Church with great splendor. A pontifical Mass with twelve visiting priests was celebrated by Bishop William Joseph Hafey of Raleigh. On that same afternoon, Bishop Hafey confirmed the jubilee confirmation class of eighty-six children and twenty adults. St. Andrew's Band played at the Hotel Roanoke for the Jubilee banquet, and, by request, the next day at the dedication of the Veterans Hospital by President Franklin D. Roosevelt.

Catholics were not only in the minority in Roanoke, but the Catholic faith was often suspect by citizens of other denominations. During a parish mission, Father Maurice, CP, took every opportunity to meet with inquirers and answer their questions. Following these sessions, the missionary priest delivered a sermon explaining beliefs and practices of Catholics, addressing some unresolved questions. St. Andrew's parish was ecumenical before that term became popular.

Our Lady of Nazareth, Roanoke
On May 22, 1929, Sister Isabel Henry died at the convent after an

illness of only four days. Sister Isabel was born in Ireland and had come to the United States forty-six years before. Her brother, Rev. J. S. Henry, arrived at noon, and funeral services were held that same day in the parish of Our Lady of Nazareth. Sisters Laurita Gibson and Anna Cecilia Brown accompanied Father Henry to Nazareth, Kentucky, where she was to be buried.

In late August, 1930, eight SCNs returned to Our Lady of Nazareth School after a summer spent in study or rest, happy to share stories and to join in the work of cleaning the convent and classrooms, both calling for attention after a two months' vacancy. On her return from Nazareth, Sister Soteris, superior at St.Andrew's, stopped to convey greetings from Mother Mary Catharine. "Even such greetings were so welcome," one of the sisters wrote, "because they always contain some spiritual thought which fills us with a new desire to rise to higher things."

In 1931, the supervisor of schools in Virginia, notified the principal that Our Lady of Nazareth was on the list of accredited schools. In 1932, the enrollment was 109 boys and 109 girls, 47 of whom were in the high school.

In early February 1931, Mother Mary Catharine granted permission for the sisters to assist the pastor, Father James Gilsenan with his missionary work in Blacksburg, Virginia. Sisters Mary Frederick and Antoniana Wilson taught religious education classes to nineteen children who awaited them every Saturday afternoon.

For eleven years, Sister Anna Cecilia, music teacher at Our Lady of Nazareth School, had been responsible for a variety of plays and musical performances presented annually by the pupils. Each recital showed marked improvement among the piano, instrumental, and choral groups. At the time of her silver jubilee, the sisters arranged for a celebration of Sister Anna Cecilia's twenty-five years in religious life and her contribution of music to the people of Roanoke.

Sacred Heart Cathedral Girls, Richmond

In 1924, enrollment at Sacred Heart Cathedral Girls' High School in Richmond, Virginia reached 420, and the school held a rank of first-class from the Virginia State Board of Education. The Cathedral Boys' School, except for the first two primary grades taught by SCNs, was under the supervision of the Xaverian Brothers

The principal, Sister Catherine Teresa Rapp, and faculty of Cathedral Girls' High enriched the students in many fields. The girls became interested in competition by writing essays, short stories and plays. Thus began the "contest" years. The topics on which they wrote show how alert and diverse were their interests. In 1930, two students distinguished themselves and their school by writing on "Chemistry in Medicine." The winning topic for the Knights of Columbus historical essay was 'The Most Critical Period in American History." The IFCA sponsored "Value of a Good Vocabulary" and the CSMC encouraged original drama competition.

Drama has long been a means of imparting knowledge, both to the cast and to the audience. Poise, diction, imagination, costume designing, period furnishings, and initiative, may be cultivated through this art. Sister Mary Adelaide Durbin, CSMC sponsor, recognized the value of writing plays to raise mission awareness. The national office of the Propagation of the Faith had published a one-act skit called "Field Afar." Spearheaded by Rose Hulcer, the sophomore class at Cathedral Girls' High added two more acts to the play and two more words to the title: "In the Field Afar." The sophomores studied pictures in the state library, designed costumes, and drew posters to advertise the play. A full house, including Bishop Andrew Brennan, and other members of the clergy, praised the young people for their creativity in advertising and in their splendid performance. The drama so held the attention of Father Walter J. Nott, Director, CSMC, Diocese of Richmond that he wrote in March 1929, to the sophomores of Cathedral Girls' High School:

> My very dear and clever children:
>
> The result of your work last night is further reaching than you imagine, for it not only instructed a number of people, but it began in this diocese original work in writing, dramatics, and advertising for the missions. This example is very useful to the cause for which you and I are so engaged . . . May God bless and keep you always near.
>
> Sincerely and with deepest appreciation,
> Walter J. Nott, Director

Father Nott asked if he might allow the play, when shared with other CSMC units, to include the changes made by the sophomores.

Mission plays became a specialty for some time. There were Lenten plays produced mainly by the junior class. The primary grades took over the Christmas season with operettas like "Busy Little Christmas Fairies," in 1931 and "The Doll's Christmas" in 1932. For class nights, the seniors had plays to finance trips, and to provide equipment for the school. Father Daniel A. Lord's compositions were favorites for class nights. His "School is Over" was declared "the finest entertainment of the 1930 senior class."

St. Vincent de Paul, Newport News

Newport News is the southernmost city on a peninsula at the mouth of the James River. The children of Navy personnel made up a significant number in St. Vincent de Paul Grade and High School. The variety of backgrounds of pupils beyond the Virginia provided a growing experience for those in Newport News. With patient understanding, the SCNs adjusted their schedules and teaching time for late-comers to St. Vincent's.

Surrounded by naval installations and shipbuilding, the sisters learned shipyard culture. One time they had a tour of an aircraft carrier under construction in the shipyard. Another time the sisters witnessed Lou Henry Hoover, wife of President Herbert Hoover, strike the bow of the ship with the ceremonial bottle of champagne and christen it "Ranger."

In 1924, a science room equipped by the St. Vincent Alumni was added to the school. During the following school year, under the direction of the principal, Sister Mary Bathildes Murphy, plans were made to build a hall, a larger school, and a convent. The music department, in December 1926, had an accomplished school orchestra that performed a holiday program.

The sisters were mindful of the needs of Catholic children living on military bases. In response to a request from Sister Mary Bathildes, Mother Mary Catharine wrote in December 1927:

> I gladly give permission for the sisters to teach catechism at Camp Eustis, and as for compensation, tell Father all we ask is that he remember us at the holy altar and should it come in his way to attract souls to our Community, that will be the greatest favor he could do us.

In 1931, the school paper "Reveille" was started. That same year enrollment in the grade school was 212. In 1932, the minimum tuition paid was $1.50 per month while the maximum tuition was $2.50. To supplement the tuition charged, expenses of the school were met by appropriations from the church budget.

On the return of the sisters in August 1931, Sister Aurelia Crump was overjoyed to tell the eight SCNs on the faculty that a chaplain had been appointed for the convent, and they would have daily Mass in their chapel.

Conclusion

At the time of Mother Mary Catharine's administration, the schools in Maryland, Massachusetts, Tennessee, and Virginia, were established institutions. She kept these schools staffed with SCNs. Mother Mary Catharine realized the value of SCN ministry in states beyond Kentucky.

Chapter Seven

Orphanages, Homes, Hospitals

St. Vincent Orphanage, Louisville, Kentucky

A century after Mother Catherine Spalding had carried abandoned infants to the convent, her name and that of the Sisters of Charity had become associated with the care of orphans. In August 1924, Sister Mary Agnita Speak succeeded Sister Antonia Byers as Superior of St. Vincent Orphanage in Louisville. School at the Orphanage began in August 1924 with an enrollment of ninety children who were taught by the sisters.

Tonsillitis was a common condition among many children of that era. Sister Mary Agnita and sisters consulted with doctors and Sister Jane Frances Heilbock, superior at Sts. Mary & Elizabeth Hospital. On December 4, 1924, Dr. W. C. White and four other physicians removed the tonsils of seventy-five children at St. Vincent Orphanage. The dental offices became the operating rooms, and the dormitory in the west wing, the patients' recovery room. Work began at 8:00 a.m. and finished at 6:30 p.m. Sister Jane Frances and Sts. Mary & Elizabeth Hospital supplied operating room equipment and three nurses. Sisters Barbara Yates and Mary Innocentia Lee came from St. Joseph's Infirmary with five night nurses and a bountiful supply of sponges. Cooperation and partnering among the medical personnel and the care-givers at St. Vincent's Orphanage made for a successful day and good health for the children.

The City of Louisville had a tradition of supporting the Fourth of July Orphans' Picnic. The picnic in 1925 surpassed all former ones. The Fourth fell on Saturday, and Bishop John A. Floersh came after midnight to offer Mass for picnic workers so that they could go home and rest on Sunday.

Mother Mary Catherine made her visitation to St. Vincent's in the spring of 1926 and saw the crowded conditions. She was relieved to receive a letter from Bishop Floersh with a proposal. He asked congregations of women religious who owned and operated academies in the diocese to accept gratis two or three girls from St. Vincent's seventh and eighth grades. SCNs at St. Frances Academy in Owensboro, and Bethlehem Academy in Bardstown, promptly agreed. The Dominican Sisters at St. Catherine's in Springfield, the Sisters of Loretto at St. John's Academy, the Ursuline Sisters at Sacred Heart Academy in Louisville, and the Sisters of Mercy at Mercy Academy in Louisville also accepted girls. As a result of this cooperation, there were no seventh or eighth grade pupils at the Orphanage for the next two years. The Orphanage Board paid for uniforms and supplies amounting to twenty-five dollars for each boarder.

In 1931, the effects of the Depression were evident when two men, assigned by the Bureau of Unemployment, came three days a week to work at the Orphanage. Carfare, lunch, and dinner were provided by the Orphanage, an arrangement that proved beneficial for all.

On June 12, 1932, a Centennial Celebration of St. Vincent and St. Thomas Orphanages was held at Columbia Auditorium in Louisville. William Melton, as spokesman for the many who had received care at the orphanages, said:

I stand before you today as a representative of the seven thousand, nine hundred and four orphans, who, during a hundred years, have found in these orphanages a home supplied by the Providence of God and by the charity of our bishops, our good sisters, and the gentlemen of the Catholic Orphan Society.

The speaker continued praising the SCNs whose congregation, during the past century, had uninterruptedly borne the responsibility of caring for homeless girls, and, often, for orphaned boys.

After an impressive program provided by children from both St. Vincent and St. Thomas Orphanages, Bishop Floersh expressed appreciation to the priests and sisters for their loyal and unwavering cooperation in this work. " I would be remiss if I did not express my deep sense of thanks to the good and beloved sisters who have so disinterestedly dedicated their lives to the care of the orphans." He thanked the countless men and women who had generously supported the work, whether as officers and members of the orphan societies, or as tireless workers at the annual picnic.

In May 1932, the orphans lost a real friend and, as young as they were, they seemed to realize it. The chaplain at St. Vincent Orphanage, Father Robert Craney, was described by the homilist at his funeral Mass as "always the same pious, upright, honorable, retiring person who never blamed others but often condemned himself. He lived to serve others, and he met death fearlessly." Sisters accompanied the seventh and eighth grade orphan girls and boys to the Cathedral for his funeral Mass.

St. Thomas Orphanage, Louisville, Kentucky

In 1910, St. Thomas Orphanage was moved permanently from Bardstown to Louisville. During the administration of Mother Mary

Catharine, Sister Lidwina Yahner (1923-29) and Sister Mary Gretchen Langenbacher (1929-35) were superiors. There were fifteen sisters on the staff for 140 boys. An elementary school on site provided grades 1-8, and there was a nursery for the younger children.

Joint celebrations of birthdays and other special occasions were arranged for the girls at St. Vincent Orphanage who had brothers at St. Thomas Orphanage. Doctors and dentists provided services free of charge. Childhood diseases, often of epidemic proportions, made great demands on generous health care providers.

Among the celebrities who visited the orphanage were: Jack Dempsey, the famous boxer; an explorer, a member of Admiral Richard E. Byrd's polar expedition; also a team of Alaskan huskies, and a pair of penguins. The radio brought an influx of national and world events. On March 4, 1933, dinner was delayed so that the boys could listen to President F.D. Roosevelt's inaugural address.

St. Peter's Orphanage, Memphis, Tennessee

Like all SCN orphanages, St. Peter's Orphanage in Memphis never lacked for means to provide for the children's spiritual and physical welfare. "St. Peter's is more like a home than an orphanage," said Father James T. Lornigan in 1927. He continued, "Some years ago, I was chaplain here for four years, and while in that position, I learned more about charity – real charity – than ever before from theologians and learned writers."

In 1927, the faithful ladies of the Sewing Club of St. Peter's Orphanage received a gift of 900 yards of outing cloth from the Good Fellows Organization, a charitable group of prominent businessmen of Memphis. The ladies made good use of the cloth, and, by working overtime, made warm nightgowns and pajamas for the children in time for Christmas. When the owner of a bakery heard that the sisters were paying one dollar a day for bread, he arranged to have their daily order of bakery goods delivered free of charge.

Children at St. Peter's Orphanage were taught by Sister Pelagia Grace and other SCNs through the eighth grade, after which, each could choose her/his high school. In 1921, Gladys Green and her siblings were brought by their father from Fancy Farm, Kentucky to St. Peter's Orphanage. After finishing school at St. Peter's, Gladys chose Sacred Heart Academy in Helena, Arkansas, where she graduated in 1925. Gladys returned to Memphis and worked as a stenographer for two years. In October 1927, she entered the novitiate of the newly-founded Foreign Mission Sisters of St. Dominic at Maryknoll, New York, and in 1933, made vows as Sister Mary Kostka Green, M.M. She spent fifty-six years in the Hawaiian Islands as a Maryknoll missionary, teacher, and principal.

The sisters at St. Peter's Orphanage wished to listen to the Holy Father speaking to the world by radio, and asked to borrow one from Colonel E.R. Bradley. His response was immediate and generous. His note read, "Keep the radio." This gift would connect the sisters with significant events of the times for years to come.

Like millions around the world in 1927, the sisters listened to President Herbert Hoover congratulate Charles A. Lindberg following his record solo flight to Paris. On Lindberg's tour in Memphis, the children cheered and waved as the mayor's limousine passed St. Peter's. With a sharp salute, Lindberg acknowledged their cheers.

In July 1928, the boys at St. Peter's could talk of little more than the upcoming Jack Dempsey/Jack Sharkey fight. To let the boys hear the blow-by-blow account, Sister Laurentilla Burns helped them move the radio into a classroom. There the voice of the announcer broadcasting from Yankee Stadium ignited the boys' excitement as they waited for the match to begin. Round after round, the boys shadow-boxed with heavy blows and swinging punches, with dancing and dodging until Dempsey finally knocked out the future heavyweight champion, Sharkey.

During the 1928 presidential election campaign, the sisters followed the speeches of Alfred E. Smith, the first Catholic candidate. Four years later, on the first Saturday of May, the sisters gathered around the radio and cheered as Colonel Bradley's horse, "Burgo King" won the 1932 Kentucky Derby. Once again, Colonel Bradley won more than the traditional blanket of roses – he won the sisters' deep gratitude for the radio.

St. Peter's Orphanage, Lowell, Massachusetts

The people of Lowell, led by the example of the Catholic laity, were faithful in meeting needs of St. Peter's Orphanage. In 1925, a city-wide picnic was held for all children's homes. It took two trucks and 103 autos to convey children to the picnic grounds.

Another example of the local support was the annual "Donation Day" for the orphans. Sister Mary Agnita Speak, with the help of the older girls, prepared their dining room as the reception place for the many gifts and donations of food, clothing, toys, and money.

Sister Mary Winifred Coomes was pleased when Mrs. Edward O'Donnell offered to share her recent trip with the sisters. She showed pictures and described her trip to the Eucharistic Congress in Dublin in 1932. To their delight, she pointed out other familiar sights, for example, a picture of herself kissing the Blarney Stone, something dear to the faithful Irish hearts.

In July 1933, a committee of four clergymen appointed by Archbishop O'Connell: Fathers Charles J. Galligan, J. P. Gill, Joseph F. Coppinger, and Joseph F. McGlinchy made an evaluation. Their report of St. Peter's Orphanage was most gratifying. It stated that the inspectors were well pleased with the institution as a whole and, in particular, with the educational and financial status.

Also in July 1933, Father Paul Russell, a cousin of Sister Teresa

Edward O'Sullivan, in charge of the boys at St. Peter's, and brother of Sister Lucille Russell, later Mother Lucille Russell, arrived from Rome where he had completed his studies for ordination. Father Paul offered his first Mass in America at St. Peter's Orphanage and gave his blessing to all. He entertained the sisters and others with accounts of his varied experiences in Rome.

St. Vincent's Home, Roanoke, Virginia

On November 19, 1931, Mother Mary Catharine sent Sisters Fidelia Nolan, Joseph Ambrose Weigan, and superior Sister Mary Pierre Byrne, to assume the work at St. Vincent Home. This relieved the double duty of the sisters teaching at St. Andrew's School by day and presiding with children in the orphanage at night. The relationships among the sisters working in both facilities remained strong as they shared the ups and downs of daily life in their respective places of ministry.

The boys of St. Vincent's Home attended St. Andrew's, the parish school, and took part in activities and functions of the school. In addition to speakers addressing the student body, visitors who stopped at the rectory were often invited to talk with the older boys to give them a picture of life beyond the orphanage. Before desegregation became the law of the land, a priest from Abyssinia soliciting on behalf of his people, called at St. Vincent's Home. The sight of a priest of color was an uncommon occurrence in Roanoke. Sister Francis Xavier Rocco invited the older boys to hear his stories and ask him questions. He spoke in a clipped British accent which the boys found both entertaining and enlightening. They had never before seen or heard a priest from Africa.

Home for Destitute Children, Newburyport, Massachusetts

Christmas decorations annually prepared at the home created a joyful spirit for the holidays. While a few children were fortunate enough to spend the day at home or with relatives, Sister Agnes Clare Laughran and the sisters planned to fill the days of Christmas with meaning and cheer for the children. A visit to the crib and singing at Mass, followed by a special dinner, prepared them for the highlight of the afternoon when they could open their gifts. The merchants of Newburyport, as well as the Knights of Columbus, Daughters of Isabella, Elks, American Legion, and other groups helped brighten the lives of the children and the sisters during the holidays.

An example of the careful, complete education provided by the SCNs at the Home occurred when, on January 2, 1927, Mr. Kelly came for his son who had been in the Home for five years. He came to place John with the Xaverian Brothers at the Guardian Angels Home. They were surprised to find John so advanced in his classes and immediately placed him in their middle grades.

On July 10, 1928, Mother Mary Catharine wrote to Cardinal O'Connell of Boston asking his permission to recall the five SCNs from the Home. "There are at present only twenty-five little girls in the Home and I understand that there are only three or four of them really dependent upon charity," she noted. In early August 1928, Sister Agnes Clare had the sad responsibility of notifying parents and guardians of the necessity of closing the Home. The sisters worked carefully to gather and clean the belongings of each child. Hiding their own feelings, they tried to keep the morale high for the children. By August 28, all had withdrawn except one older girl who stayed to help until she left on Labor Day for the home in Lawrence, Massachusetts.

One challenging, time-consuming task fell upon Sister Mary Dominica Clements who was in charge of the supply room at the Home. Her unfailing foresight in providing generously for hungry children left her with a sizable inventory of supplies worth over five hundred dollars. The superiors in Hyde Park, Brockton, Lynn, and Lowell purchased some of the food. The Christian Brothers, who were opening a new home for boys in West Newbury, took the remainder of the canned goods and many things they could use in their new facility.

The Home for Destitute Children, after thirty-six years of service was closed on September 14, 1928. One week later, a letter from Mother Mary Catharine warmly welcomed the Newburyport Sisters back to Nazareth. Ever thoughtful and kind, Mother assured them that they should rest at Nazareth before starting in a new field of labor.

St. Theresa House, Lynn, Massachusetts

St. Theresa House was the "dream realized" by Msgr. Arthur J. Teeling, pastor of St. Mary Church in Lynn, Massachusetts to offer safe, comfortable, attractive housing for young business women. Msgr. Teeling had first heard of the SCNs from Father Michael Ronan, who had studied at St. Thomas Seminary near Bardstown, Kentucky. At Msgr. Teeling's request, SCNs staffed the facility from its opening in 1918. The forty-two rooms were quickly filled, and a waiting list was continuous.

Sister Mary Edward Phelan's second term as superior was shortened because of illness, and she was succeeded by Sister Innocentia Meagher. When Sister Innocentia died in 1929, Sister Mary Pierre Byrne was appointed Superior. She carried out extensive improvements planned by Sister Innocentia.

In June 1931, Msgr. J. F. McGlinchey of St. Mary's Parish informed Sister Mary Pierre that, with the Cardinal's permission, the pastor wished SCNs to withdraw. He wanted the Diocesan Sisters of St. Joseph (SSJ) to take charge, explaining that the SSJs now teaching in the new parish high school for boys, had no home. He further stated that SCNs took charge of St. Theresa Home to please

Msgr. Teeling who had died in 1927. He added that it was not the usual SCN ministry. After thirteen years of operation, SCNs left St. Theresa's on July 31, 1931. Young women from St. Mary's Parish in Lynn who became SCNs were Sisters Walter Ann Kane, Margaret Edward Noon, and Norma Alexander.

O'Leary Home for Men, Louisville, Kentucky
Mother Mary Catharine, always concerned about the well-being of the poor, wrote to Sister Mary George Lancaster, superior at O'Leary Home for Men, located on Barrett Avenue in Louisville. She asked whether one more indigent could be admitted. Sister Mary George replied that accommodations at the home comprised space for ten men and four sisters. She regretted that they had no more room at present. Before Sister Mary George left O'Leary Home in 1932, Mother Mary Catharine wrote her a note of appreciation: "Your long years of faithful, loyal service to our dear community, and your spirit of obedience and submission are lessons for emulation by your sisters."

In this period of history, ethnicity was such a social issue that separate provisions were arranged. Sacred Heart Home, conducted by the Sisters of Mercy, cared for men of German extraction. Most of the occupants at O'Leary Home were Irish, and they celebrated traditional Irish holidays.

On October 20, 1933, Sister Macaria Scott, well known for sixteen years of generous service at O'Leary Home, died. Records show that Sister Macaria had spent two years nursing the sick at St. John's Eruptive Hospital in Louisville, caring for victims of small pox. Sister nursed victims of the "dread disease" elsewhere at St. Clara's Academy in Yazoo City, Mississippi, and at Immaculata Academy in Newport, Kentucky. Despite her diminishing eyesight, Sister Macaria continued her ministry as a housekeeper for many years at O'Leary Home.

St. Joseph Infirmary, Louisville, Kentucky

In 1919, St. Joseph's Infirmary opened a school of nursing with seven sisters as their first students. The following year, seven lay students were admitted. In the mid-twenties, the total number in the training school was eighteen. First and second year lectures were given by physicians and sister nurses at the hospital. In the third and fourth years, students attended classes at the Medical School of the University of Louisville. The spiritual development of the nursing students was essential to their training, and included courses in medical ethics, an annual retreat, and regular meetings of the Sodality of Our Lady.

On January 10, 1925, Mother Mary Catharine called an emergency meeting of her council along with Sisters Evangelista Malone, Marietta Murphy, and Mother Rose Meagher, to consider changing the name from St. Joseph's Infirmary to St. Joseph's Hospital. Some doctors and other medical personnel considered "hospital" the proper word for the medical facility. After deliberation, the sisters decided that the ministry of St. Joseph's Infirmary was so well known by its present name that a change would be of no benefit. The council was unanimous in agreement to retain the name, St. Joseph's Infirmary, the one first used by Mother Catherine Spalding when she began the ministry of health care in Louisville.

Soon after the renovation of St. Vincent de Paul Church at Nazareth in 1925, Mother Mary Catharine faced another significant challenge. St. Joseph Infirmary located on South Fourth Street, the site to which Mother Catherine Spalding had relocated it, had outgrown its size. Three times as many beds were required to care for the ever-increasing number of patients.

A special meeting of the Nazareth Literary and Benevolent Institute, was held on December 21, 1925, at Nazareth, to accept the proposal of the Fidelity and Columbia Trust Company to purchase

St. Joseph Infirmary on Fourth Street for $1,250,000.

The annals call May 31, 1926, "a never-to-be-forgotten day in the history of St. Joseph's Infirmary." Early in the morning the great move began. St. Joseph's, with an accumulation of many years, was to be cleared out. Sisters, student nurses, and patients were to sleep in the new infirmary that night. The new structure on Eastern Parkway had a 345 bed capacity.

With her usual trust in Divine Providence, Mother Mary Catharine had the courage to build the expansive edifice of St. Joseph's Infirmary on Eastern Parkway. Newspaper accounts referred to the new building as "handsome, almost like a castle." As her predecessor, Mother Catherine Spalding's reply to her critics of 1822 that the halls of Nazareth would one day be filled proved to be prophetic, so would the five stories of St. Joseph's Infirmary. In actuality, its capacity would become insufficient to meet increasing demands, and soon after its completion, plans were underway to construct an additional wing.

The *Herald Post* of Louisville in 1926 posed a question that might well be asked today:

> Did Mother Catherine Spalding, who began this great work with a humble beginning in 1836 and later in 1853 (the real foundation of St. Joseph Infirmary), ever dream that in less than three quarters of a century the needs of Louisville would require an institution such as the present one?

In their coverage of the new St. Joseph Infirmary, *The Record* paid this tribute to SCNs:

> Their ministrations in the name of charity have been a blessing to the sick and the old and the poor for nearly one hundred years. Their achievement, which is a notable contribution to

the fame of our city, a living testimonial of their unfaltering service, and the hope that never dies, is synonymous with the name of Nazareth.

Sts. Mary & Elizabeth Hospital, Louisville, Kentucky

In 1924, Sts. Mary & Elizabeth Hospital celebrated its Golden Jubilee. To keep the occasion simple, the sisters invited only Father William Hogarty of New Haven, Kentucky, to celebrate Mass. Father Hogarty was chosen because, as a young priest at the Cathedral of the Assumption in Louisville, he had been present when the building was first blessed on January 6, 1874. One sister in the group, Sister Regis McKeigney, told the story of that feast of the Epiphany when she witnessed the first blessing and dedication of the hospital. Later in the afternoon, Bishop John A. Floersh honored the sisters with a special visit.

As in other SCN nursing schools, a Sodality of Our Lady was organized in 1924. The philosophy of the nurses training school at Sts. Mary & Elizabeth Hospital appeared in the 1920s in the *Bulletin* of the Hospital.

> The object of the Sisters in conducting the Training School is to form young women, possessed of the necessary qualifications to do the noble, self-sacrificing and delicate duty of caring for the sick in an intelligent manner. . . . While the institution is conducted by the Catholic Sisterhood, the question of Creed never enters into the work, either as to patient or the selection of the students in the training school.

In 1926, Sister Mary Boniface Schum, a graduate of the Training School, was appointed to the Nurses' State Board of Examiners. That same year, five nurses in training began to take courses toward an RN at Nazareth College, Louisville. Fifty-one young women attended the Training School in 1932. In accordance with Canon Law, Mother Mary Catharine requested Bishop Floersh's permission to send sisters to study at the University of Louisville. Sisters Crescentia Wise, Anne Snow, and Margaret Ann Schwering studied pharmacy, and Sisters Crescentia and Anne were subsequently in charge of the pharmacy at Sts. Mary & Elizabeth Hospital.

In 1920, Sts. Mary & Elizabeth Hospital received a religious painting of the Visitation donated by Edwin B. Bacon of J. Bacon & Sons, the oldest dry goods company in Louisville. The hospital was named in honor of Mary Eliza Breckenridge, the wife of its donor, William Shakespeare Caldwell. The painting depicts a welcoming exchange between Mary and Elizabeth when Mary visited her cousin to assist in her time of need. For years the painting hung on the side wall of the front hall of the hospital, its beauty hidden to passersby. In 1928, it was moved to a prominent place on the second floor.

On Oct. 4, 1929, nine victims of the L&N railroad wreck at Stanford, Kentucky, were brought to the hospital. One was an African-American porter. The charter of Sts. Mary & Elizabeth (1874) stating that no "Negroes" would be accepted as patients had been stipulated by William Shakespeare Caldwell, the major donor of the hospital. The sisters on the medical staff saw to it that the porter received the very best treatment for his injuries and accommodations for the night. The next day, he was transferred to the Red Cross Hospital in Louisville.

Mount St. Agnes Sanitarium, Louisville, Kentucky

To care for the sisters with mental needs, the Congregation purchased forty-four acres of scenic property on Newburg Road from Bishop Denis O'Donaghue of Louisville for the sum of $15,000. On the property were two dwellings, both in need of repair. Nazareth renovated the houses at a cost of $9,600, and another small dwelling was also repaired for the care-takers of St. Agnes.

Sister Mary Benigna Heslin was placed in charge with Sisters Letitia Finley and Emily Thompson on staff. Spiritual ministry was provided by the Passionist priests whose monastery was located on property adjoining Mount St. Agnes. In September 1924, Sister Mary Cassilda Stey arrived at Mount St. Agnes as superior. With foresight in administration, she suggested at a board meeting that they establish a system of charts, records, and histories of the patients. The Board did not accept the proposal.

Joy comes in different places and colors. Such was the case in 1933, when Sister Jane Frances Heilbock, superior at Mt. St. Agnes, talked with Mother Mary Catharine about the need to brighten up walls, ceilings, and trim of the annex. Recalling the "nest egg" recently increased by generous jubilee gifts, Mother Mary Catharine unhesitatingly directed, "Brighten it up!"

St. Joseph's Hospital, Lexington, Kentucky

The feast of Our Lady of Lourdes, February 11, 1929, was a memorable one for St. Joseph's Hospital and for the entire city of Lexington. In temperatures of minus 13 degrees, the sisters, having made their last visits to their assigned floors, retired for the night. As they walked toward the nurses' home across the street from the hospital, two sisters saw a woman hurrying across the lawn pointing to the attic, calling out, "Isn't that a fire up there?" In seconds, the alarm spread by phone to the City Fire Department, to the two hundred Knights of Columbus at dinner at the K of C Hall, and to the nurses attending a dance. The response was immediate among clergy, professionals, and countless citizens of Lexington.

Within forty minutes, ambulances from five funeral establishments arrived to move the 118 patients to temporary locations. The most critically ill were received at Good Samaritan Hospital. Others were sent to the new Julius Marx Sanitarium, not yet operational. Some patients went to St. Catherine Academy, others to the nurses' home, and some to private homes.

As fire spread through the building, Sister Mary Sebastian Schimanski, in charge of the kitchen, found it undisturbed. She and other sisters made sandwiches and coffee for the firemen and other workers whose water soaked garments had frozen. The Phoenix Hotel also sent sandwiches and coffee. For three days after the fire, the Phoenix and two other local hotels continued to send food. Mrs. Nannie Feeney, an invalid for many years, kept the Blessed Sacrament in her home across the street from the hospital.

The day after the fire, Mother Mary Catharine arrived to console the sisters and to offer them her assistance. She advised that SCN patients be moved to St. Joseph Infirmary in Louisville. In two days time, a local construction company was contracted to restore and modernize the destroyed sections. Lexington women helped clear debris from water soaked areas and soon restored those sections to use. Within forty-eight hours, forty patients had returned to St. Joseph's, and the regular round of duties resumed under a temporary roof while the work of reconstruction proceeded. Fundraising to restore the hospital began immediately. Donations, small and large, came from many sources, and St. Joseph Hospital rose from the ashes. Three years after the fire, June 23, 1932, The *Lexington Herald* reported:

> St Joseph Hospital has kept pace with the advancements in modern Medicine and is proud of the excellent doctors who make up its staff; that they are progressive and truly scientific is well known by those in charge of the hospital; that the patient is first and foremost in everyone's consideration... permeates the entire atmosphere of this institution.

The Training School for Nurses began in 1918. *The Circular of Information,* an early St. Joseph Hospital publication, stated its philosophy:

> While it is the purpose of the school to give nursing students an education that will place them in the front rank of skilled nurses and make them self-sustaining by this honorable profession, it is also the aim to enlist the interest and efforts of intelligent, well-educated ladies in the care of the sick.

Tuition and board were free. Each student, after a probation period of six months, was given an allowance of five dollars a month. In September 1932, the school had seventy-six student nurses, and the number of patients cared for during the year was 4,690.

Mercy Hospital, Mt. Vernon, Ohio

In 1930, Rev. Alphonse Schwitalli, S.J., president of the Catholic Hospital Association (CHA), wrote to Mother Mary Catharine inquiring whether Mercy Hospital could be incorporated into CHA membership. In reply Mother said, "Mercy is a small hospital in a small town with no nurses training school and cannot qualify for membership in CHA now." She added, "Mercy Hospital is nevertheless doing splendid service, especially in the way of breaking down prejudices among the many non-Catholics of that section of Ohio."

To the satisfaction of Mercy Hospital and citizens of Mt. Vernon, a surgeon joined the staff in 1933. As word circulated of his residency there, confidence of the people in Knox County was strengthened since patients could receive care in Mt. Vernon. In 1934, Mother Mary Catharine approved the renovation of the building to further adapt it for service as a hospital.

One day, a nurse, known for keeping up with innovations, came to the administrator carrying a new catalog with pages marked. Sister Mary Cassilda Stey was not surprised that her requests included, along with the latest in medical supplies, a mobile Kel-Ket X-ray machine, a new Hoover sweeper to lighten the work in the recently enlarged hospital, and an additional order for rubber gloves. The latter had been on the market only a short time and were now in the catalogs. Before that, it was "bare hands!"

By 1936, increasing numbers of patients needing immediate treatment were being brought to Mercy Hospital. Emergency decisions had to be made. Returning from retreat, Sister Rose Edna Higdon, Head of the X-ray Department, found her room occupied by a patient. Her bed and belongings had been moved to the attic with other sisters to make room for patients.

On March 10, 1936, the Maternity Department of Mercy Hospital celebrated a red-letter day when five babies were born in twenty-four hours, one being the first African American baby delivered at Mercy Hospital.

St. Vincent's Infirmary, Little Rock, Arkansas

An article in the *Arkansas Times* on April 24, 1926, recalled that St. Vincent Infirmary had been established over a quarter of a century before in Little Rock by Sisters of Charity of Nazareth:

> They came – a well-organized and trained corps ready to relieve the sick, maimed, and dying. This began a welfare work for Little Rock, which proved to be a veritable god-send for the past 38 years.

With confidence in the hospitality and thorough preparations of SCNs and staff at St. Vincent Infirmary, Sister Michaella Duke, superior, hosted a meeting of the Southern Conference of the Catholic Hospital Association in November 1924. Commenting on the merits of that convention, the reporter noted that St. Vincent Infirmary had provided a program attractive to executives and valuable to hospital personnel from neighboring states.

In 1906, St. Vincent Infirmary had the distinction of being the first SCN hospital to open a training school for nurses. In addition to the classes in nursing, an annual retreat was available to Catholics and non-Catholics alike. The Training School established an alumnae association whose stated purpose was to "maintain a loyal adherence of its members to the highest principles of their noble profession." In 1932, there were sixty nurses in training.

For seven years, Sister Mary Paul Corby had served as director of medical records at St. Vincent's Infirmary, and as assistant supervisor of nurses. In addition, a particular success of Sister Mary Paul should not be overlooked. Besides supervising medical records, she was responsible for *St.Vincent's Bulletin*, and relied heavily upon articles written by the doctors describing successes or failures in their departments. Forthright description of a failed procedure may have prevented its repetition at St. Vincent's and other medical facilities. Similarly, a recorded success could not only encourage medical personnel but also contribute to the growth of the body of tested medical knowledge.

When some staff members had suggested stopping altogether the publication of *St. Vincent's Bulletin*, Sister Mary Paul faithfully kept it alive. In a succeeding issue she wrote:

> Ethical medical institutions become distinctive and medical personnel become famous because of the work they do. Results of their good work become known in two ways. First, good work means satisfied patients, and satisfied patients spread the news in their home communities so that other patients come and leave, spreading the good news. Thus in an ever-widening circle, the reputation of a good surgeon or a good institution, or a city in which good medical work is done, is spread. Second, the result of work carefully done is

reported in articles contributed to medical publications and sent to physicians so that others may profit. Every nationally known physician and/or hospital is famous, not from their work alone, but because their work has been publicized.

Hoping to convince the doctors to continue to contribute to *St. Vincent's Bulletin*, Sister Mary Paul added this touching story:

> My baby brother, then a boy of four, had been caught by his mother in some sort of mischief. In scolding him, she said, "What do you think I should do to you?" He replied, "Keep me." Keep him – for what he was, and for what he would become. The boy grew up to be an electrical engineer. . .

Publication of the professional journal continued.

Conclusion

SCNs are always women of their time. By the mid 1930s, the end of Mother Mary Catharine's term of office, they had moved with the nation from an agrarian way of life to a more industrialized one. The full life and ministry of the Sisters of Charity of Nazareth during the administration of Mother Mary Catharine Malone cannot be contained within the limits of these pages. The spirit of the congregation at this time carried the sisters through difficult and challenging situations. When searching for the daily strength that inspired their dedicated service, one must conclude that the sisters were indeed "impelled by the love of Christ."

Afterword

Mother Mary Catharine Malone's gift of joy was a trademark of her character as was her sensitivity to the needs of others. Elected Mother General in 1924, she served twelve years in that office. Mother Mary Catharine accomplished much during her two terms, and, as historical evidence testifies, was an effective leader of the community.

Mother's leadership occurred during a period of active patriotism in the United States. World War I had ended, and the patriotism it fostered continued. Mother's awareness of the rights and privileges of citizenship was evident in her circular letter to the sisters written in 1924:

> We think it would be well for every sister to become a naturalized citizen of this country which is our home, and which gives us protection and the privilege of using the ballot for the promotion of good government and as a defense against unjust laws. However, no one will be urged to do so against her will.

Mother Mary Catharine's devotion to rural and immigrant families endure as part of her legacy. Where language barriers affected the spiritual and civic life of immigrants, she provided multilingual sisters. Impoverished parishes during the time of the Depression were unable to pay sisters' salaries. She did not withdraw the sisters but continued the SCN commitment to education. When Kentucky began to focus its educational efforts on cities due to their rising population, Mother Mary Catharine was especially attentive to rural education.

Mother Mary Catharine's administration ended in 1936. Five years later, on August 27, 1941, after an illness of only a few hours, she died at Nazareth at age eighty. Her funeral was attended by five bishops, forty clergy, and five hundred SCNs, attesting to the high esteem and affection in which she was held. A Nazareth annalist described her death as "the grand finale of the beautiful symphony of her long life."

Timeline

In the list below, "Sisters of Charity" or SCN will always indicate the Sisters of Charity of Nazareth, Kentucky. "Louisville" will always indicate Louisville, Kentucky.

1924   General Chapter elects Mother Mary Catharine Malone.

Expansion of St. Vincent Church begins.

Nuns of the Battlefield Memorial Monument erected in Washington, D.C.

St Charles, Bardwell, KY; Our Lady's, Medley's Neck, MD; St. Joseph, Morganza, MD; St. Gregory, Samuels, KY, schools opened.

Sts. Mary & Elizabeth Hospital, Louisville 50th jubilee

1925   Infantile paralysis epidemic closes Louisville schools.

St. Joseph Infirmary, Louisville moved to Eastern Parkway.

St. Joseph Colored School, Morganza, MD opened.

1926   St. Joseph School, Circleville, OH closed.

Sacred Heart, Bushwood, Holy Angels, Avenue, MD schools opened.

The Life of J.B.M. David, by Columba Fox, SCN published.

Rev. Joseph Meany, MM, 1st beneficiary of Mother Catherine Spalding burse.

Msgr. Dominic Langenbacher, C.P. requests SCNs to go to China.

1927   All grades below the 7th discontinued at Nazareth Academy.

Sister Martina Moynihan, 1st assistant to Mother Mary Catharine dies.

Sister Dorothea Creeden elected to fill the vacancy on the SCN Council.

1928   Catholic Colored High School, Louisville, opened.

Sixty apple trees set out on Nazareth hillside.

First retreat for laywomen held at Nazareth.

Diamond Jubilee of Nazareth Sodality.

Sisters staff Balltown public school in Nelson County, KY.

1929   Ignatius Hall, new gymnasium, built at Nazareth.

Nazareth becomes agency for ticket sales for L&N Railroad.

Disastrous fire at St. Joseph Hospital, Lexington, KY.

Home for Destitute Children, Newburyport, MA, closed.

Sisters staff public schools in Nelson County, KY: Culvertown and Sutherland.

1930   Mother Mary Catharine Malone reelected for six years.

Outdoor stations erected on the walk to cemetery.

Mother Rose Meagher dies on Nov. 2.

1931   Presentation Academy celebrates centennial.

Mother Mary Catharine celebrates golden jubilee.

St. Theresa Home for Working Women, Lynn, MA, closed.

1932 St. Vincent School, New Hope, KY becomes public school, SCNs continue to staff.

Rev. Patrick Donnelly, MM, recipient of Mother Catherine Spalding burse, ordained and sent to China.

Immaculata Academy in Newport, KY, closed and grade school becomes parochial.

1933 SCN Congregation sends congratulations to the Sisters of Charity of Leavenworth on the 75th anniversary of their "going west."

S. Lauretta Maher, last of the SCN Civil War nurses, dies.

1934 Fire at Bushwood Manor destroys convent of sisters teaching at Avenue and at Bushwood.

St. Teresa School, Rhodelia, KY becomes Meade County Public School, sisters continue to staff.

Celebration of centenary of Catholicity in Roanoke, VA.

1935 Rev. James P. McGee becomes assistant to Father Davis, chaplain at Nazareth.

St. Jerome School in Fancy Farm, KY becomes a Graves County Public School, sisters continue as teachers.

Fire at Bethlehem Convent, Bardstown, KY.

1936 Nazareth establishes a burse of $6,000 for the education of priests for the Diocese of Louisville.

Sister Mary Stephen supervises the extraction of a ton of honey from Nazareth's beehives.

106 sisters participate in the General Chapter held in July; Mother Ann Sebastian Sullivan elected fourth Mother General.

Mothers Superior

Catherine Spalding: 1813-1819, 1824-1831, 1838-1844, 1850-1856
Agnes Higdon: 1819-1824
Angela Spink: 1831-1832
Frances Gardiner: 1832-1838, 1844-1850, 1856-1862, 1868-1874
Columba Carroll: 1862-1868, 1874-1878
Helena Tormey: 1879-1885, 1891-1897
Cleophas Mills: 1885-1891, 1897-1903
Alphonsa Kerr: 1903-1909
Eutropia McMahon: 1909-1911

Mothers General

Eutropia McMahon 1911-1912
Rose Meagher 1912-1924
Mary Catharine Malone 1924-1936

SCN General Council 1924-1930

Mother Mary Catharine Malone
Martina Moynihan, 1st Assistant, d. 1927
Mary Ignatius Fox, 2nd Assistant
Mary Stephen Durbin, 3rd Assistant
Dorothea Creeden, 4th Assistant 1927-1930
Mary Joseph Ryan, Secretary
Evangelista Malone, Treasurer

SCN General Council 1930-1936

Mother Mary Catharine Malone
Ann Sebastian Sullivan, 1st Assistant
Mary John Horrell, 2nd Assistant
Mary Stephen Durbin, 3rd Assistant
Bertrand Crimmins, 4th Assistant and Secretary General
Evangelista Malone, Treasurer

1936 Statistics of SCN Institutions

Academies Owned-Staffed by the Sisters of Charity of Nazareth

Statistics from the The Official Catholic Directory 1936

KENTUCKY

Opened	Academy	Location	SCNs	+Lay	Pupils
1814	Nazareth*	Nazareth	27	3	166
1819	Bethlehem	Bardstown	16		330
1820	St. Vincent	Union County	20		125
1823	St. Catherine	Lexington	17		275
1831	Presentation	Louisville	21		295
1849	St. Frances	Owensboro	21		515
1856	La Salette	Covington	26	1	255
1857	Immaculata	Newport	13		226
1858	St. Mary	Paducah	17		505
1870	St. Theresa**	Rhodelia	2		56

ARKANSAS

Opened	Academy	Location	SCNs	+Lay	Pupils
1879	Sacred Heart	Helena	14		235
1880	Annunciation	Pine Bluff	7		123

MARYLAND

Opened	Academy	Location	SCNs	+Lay	Pupils
1885	St. Mary's	Leonardtown	21		220

MISSISSIPPI

Opened	Academy	Location	SCNs	+Lay	Pupils
1871	St. Clara	Yazoo City	8		136

Statistics-Nazareth Academy/Junior College combined in The Official Catholic Directory 1936
**became a parochial school in 1926*

Colleges Owned-Staffed by the Sisters of Charity of Nazareth

KENTUCKY

Opened	College	Location	SCNs	+Lay	Students
1913	St. Helena Commercial	Louisville	18	2	235
1920	Nazareth	Louisville	20	9	461
1921	Nazareth Junior*	Nazareth	11	2	166

Statistics are taken from The Official Catholic Directory 1936
*Statistics for Nazareth Junior College/Academy combined

Parochial Schools Staffed by Sisters of Charity of Nazareth

Statistics are taken from The Official Catholic Directory 1936
(NB: +1, +2, etc., under faculty, indicates lay teachers; hs indicates high school)

KENTUCKY

Opened	School	Location	Faculty	Pupils
1856	St. Mary	Covington	6	309
1857	St. Patrick	Covington	6	317
1857	St. Patrick	Louisville	6	261
1861	Good Shepherd (orig. St. Joseph Acad.)	Frankfort	7	201
1862	St. John	Louisville	4	195
1863	St. Joseph (orig. St. Columba Acad.)	Bowling Green	5	112
1867	St. Michael	Louisville	2	52
1870	St. Theresa	Rhodelia	4	56
1871	St. Monica	Bardstown	2	78
1871	St. Augustine	Louisville	6+1	260
1872	St. Agnes (orig. St. Rose Acad.)	Uniontown	8	275
1872	Holy Name	Henderson	9	258
1874	St. Brigid	Louisville	9	313
1876	St. Cecilia	Louisville	17	876
1877	Sacred Heart	Louisville	8	284
1887	St. Frances of Rome	Louisville	7	310

1887	St. Paul	Lexington	5	208
1888	St. Mary	Paris	3	53
1888	St. Peter Claver	Lexington	2	81
1891	Holy Name	Louisville	19	936
1892	St. Jerome+hs	Fancy Farm	9	355
1893	St. Anthony	Bellevue	7	265
1893	St. James+hs	Ludlow	4	254
1899	St. Philip Neri	Louisville	7	279
1900	St. Vincent de Paul+hs	New Hope	4	190
1901	St. Mary of the Woods+hs	Whitesville	6	209
1909	St. Mildred	Somerset	3	49
1912	St. Ann	Morganfield	6	154
1914	St. Thomas*	Bardstown	3	60
1914	St. Agnes	Louisville	4	194
1915	St. Peter	Lexington	5	200
1928	Catholic Colored High (orig. St. Augustine HS)	Louisville	2	67
1923	Holy Family	Louisville	5	201
1924	St. Gregory	Samuels	2	4

*closed in 1931, statistics from earlier source

Nelson County, Kentucky Public Schools Staffed by Sisters of Charity of Nazareth

Opened	School	Location	Faculty	Pupils
1928	Balltown	Balltown	2	60
1929	Sutherland	Near Bardstown	2	70
1929	Culvertown	Culvertown	2	70

Statistics are taken from The Official Catholic Directory 1936
(NB: +1, +2, etc., under faculty, indicates lay teachers; hs indicates high school)

MASSACHUSETTS

Opened	School	Location	Faculty	Pupils
1882	Immaculate Conception	Newburyport	13	462
1887	St. Patrick	Brockton	19	625
1888	St. Raphael	Hyde Park	22+2	1050
	includes St. Catherine, Corriganville)			
1912	St.Eulalia/Nazareth/St. Brigid	South Boston	26+6	1041
1922	St. Anne	Readville	8+1	323

MARYLAND

Opened	School	Location	Faculty	Pupils
1923	St. John	Hollywood	4	130
1924	St. Joseph	Morganza	3	125
1924	Our Lady's	Medley's Neck	2	100
1925	St. Joseph Colored	Morganza	2	76
1926	Holy Angels	Avenue	3	133
1926	Sacred Heart	Bushwood	2+1	80

OHIO

Opened	School	Location	Faculty	Pupils
1879	St. John+hs	Bellaire	13+1	771
1884	St. Vincent de Paul+hs	Mount Vernon	8	287
1886	St. Joseph	Circleville	4	52
1888	St. Bernard+hs	Corning	8	250
1889	St. Mary+hs	Martins Ferry	10+2	403
1891	St. Anthony	Bridgeport	7	285
1891	St. Mary+hs	Shawnee	5	112
1891	Immaculate Conception+hs	Dennison	7	418
1898	St. Stanislaus	Maynard	5	272
1904	Holy Angels	Barton	5	214
1910	St. Joseph	Wolfhurst	4	247
1914	St. Dominic	Columbus	8	340
1922	Our Lady of Victory +hs	Columbus	6	279

TENNESSEE

Opened	School	Location	Faculty	Pupils
1870	St. Brigid	Memphis	4	169
1884	St. Patrick	Memphis	3	102
1900	Sacred Heart+hs	Memphis	17	650
1930	Little Flower	Memphis	8	350
1900	Sacred Heart+hs	Memphis	17	650
1930	Little Flower	Memphis	8	350

VIRGINIA

Opened	School	Location	Faculty	Pupils
1893	St. Andrew+hs	Roanoke	11	477
1901	Cathedral of Sacred Heart+hs	Richmond	14	332
1903	St. Vincent de Paul+hs	Newport News	9	260
1916	Our Lady of Nazareth+hs	Roanoke	9	195

Statistics are taken from The Official Catholic Directory 1936

Orphanages Staffed by the Sisters of Charity of Nazareth

Statistics taken from The Official Catholic Directory 1936

KENTUCKY

Opened	Orphanage	Location	SCNs	Children
1832	St. Vincent	Louisville	18	100
1850	St. Thomas *(founded in Bardstown)*	Louisville	15	118

MASSACHUSETTS

Opened	Orphanage	Location	SCNs	Children
1887	St. Peter Orphanage	Lowell	9	135
1892	Home for Destitute Children	Newburyport	5	5

TENNESSEE

Opened	Orphanage	Location	SCNs	Children
1852	St. Peter's *(SCNs assumed staffing in 1886)*	Memphis	19	191

VIRGINIA

Opened	Orphanage	Location	SCNs	Children
1893	St. Vincent Home	Roanoke	4	48

Homes for Adults Staffed by the Sisters of Charity of Nazareth

Statistics taken from The Official Catholic Directory 1936. *If not included in the OCD 1936, the information came from convent annals or was estimated*

KENTUCKY

Opened	Home	Location	SCNS	Adults
1898 (1990)	O'Leary Home	Louisville (KY)	4	9
1918	St. Theresa Home	Lynn (MA)	6	50

Hospitals Owned and Staffed by the Sisters of Charity of Nazareth

Statistics taken from The Official Catholic Directory 1936. *If not included in the OCD 1936, the information came from convent annals or was estimated*

KENTUCKY

Opened	Orphanage	Location	SCNs	Patients
1836	St. Joseph Infirmary	Louisville	57	5731
(1919)	School of Nursing			
	75 Student Nurses			
1874	Sts. Mary & Elizabeth	Louisville	42	2800
(1915)	School of Nursing			
	50 Student Nurses			
1877	St. Joseph Hospital	Lexington	52	5109
(1918)	School of Nursing			
	65 Student Nurses			
1913	Mount St. Agnes	Louisville	25	23

(Several SCN teachers lived in residence–only SCNs were patients.)

ARKANSAS

Opened	Orphanage	Location	SCNs	Patients
1888	St. Vincent Infirmary	Little Rock	20	3489
(1906)	School of Nursing			
	65 Student Nurses			

OHIO

Opened	Orphanage	Location	SCNs	Patients
1919	Our Lady of Mercy	Mt. Vernon	8	962

Index

Murphy, Honor 53

Patricia Kelley, SCN

Patricia Kelley, a native of Lexington, KY, entered the SCN congregation in 1940. From her school days at Nazareth, Patricia knew Mother Mary Catharine Malone as an ever-welcoming person. After receiving a degree in Education, Sister Patricia taught in Louisville. In 1952, she joined the SCNs in India. Teaching at Nazareth Academy in Gaya prepared her for the next phase of her missionary life: twenty years spent in recruitment and religious formation of young women in the SCN congregation's newly established novitiate in India. Sister Patricia saw the India region of six sisters grow into a province of two hundred SCNs. Returning to the United States in 1977, she continued missionary education through writing and by visiting schools. Her book, *Fifty Monsoons*, (1999) showcases changes brought about among and through Indian women of various castes.

Rachel Willet, SCN

Rachel Willett, a native of Fancy Farm, KY, studied twelve years with the Sisters of Charity of Nazareth and grew to admire "the life and ministries of SCNs." After graduation in 1939, she began studies at Nazareth College with an English major in mind, while including two practical business courses. Subsequently, Rachel enjoyed a three year secretarial experience at Sperti, Inc. in Cincinnati, OH. In 1942, Rachel entered the SCN novitiate, receiving the name, "Sister Jerome." After profession of vows in 1944, she began a forty-year teaching/administration career chiefly on secondary and college levels. Her years of teaching dove-tailed with studies for the master's degree in English at Notre Dame University, South Bend, IN and further course work at both Oxford and London universities in England. In 1982, Sister Rachel served as secretary to Most Reverend John J. McRaith, Bishop of Owensboro, KY, and to SCN Presidents Emily Nabholz and Elizabeth Wendeln.

"The love of Christ impels us."
(2Cor. 5:14)

The pelican was chosen in early Christian times as a symbol of Christ's self-giving love on the cross and in the Eucharist. The choice was based on a legend that the mother pelican feeds her young with blood from a wound she makes in her breast when no food is available.

The quotation, "The love of Christ impels us," was used so consistently by St. Louise de Marillac and St. Vincent de Paul that it became the motto of the first Daughters of Charity. It is also the motto of the Sisters of Charity of Nazareth, who were founded in 1812 and follow the Rule of St. Vincent de Paul. The pelican is a fitting symbol of this scriptural text.

When, in 1830, Mother Catherine Spalding, Bishop Flaget and Bishop David were given the mandate to design a seal for the SCN legal corporation, Nazareth Literary and Benevolent Institution (NLBI), they naturally chose the pelican surrounded by the corporation title. The Sisters of Charity of Nazareth have an unbroken tradition of combining the motto and the essential design of this original seal, adapting it for specific uses. In this series of books on the history of the second century of the SCN community, this tradition continues.